Why Scottish Literature Matters

WHY SCOTTISH LITERATURE MATTERS

Carla Sassi

THE SALTIRE SOCIETY

Why Scottish Literature Matters
published 2005 by

The Saltire Society
9 Fountain Close,
22 High Street,
Edinburgh EH1 1TF

A catalogue record for this book is available
from the British Library.

ISBN 0 85411 082 8

Scottish
Arts Council

The publisher is very grateful to the Scottish Arts Council
for financial assistance in the publication of this book

Cover Design by James Hutcheson
Printed and Bound in Scotland by Bell and Bain Limited

alla scozia

Contents

Acknowledgements

This book is the outcome of several years of research and teaching activity, it is therefore impossible to record here all those — friends and colleagues — who indirectly contributed, with their response to my work and ideas and with their support, to its making. Among these I would like to remember Hamish Henderson, Sorley MacLean and Tom Scott: it was through the study of their work and their friendship that I was encouraged to undertake this field of studies, in the early 1990s.

For taking the time to read my manuscript, or sections of it, and coming back to me with most valuable comments I wish to thank first and foremost Ian Brown, Robert Alan Jamieson, Christopher Whyte and Patrick Williams. Douglas Dunn, Joy Hendry, Tom Hubbard, Aonghas MacNeacail, Bill Malcolm, John Manson and Claus Pollner also provided, at different stages, relevant information as well as an inspiring exchange of ideas on Scottish literary matters. For support and encouragement in my Scottish studies undertakings, extended over the years, I am grateful especially to Douglas Dunn and Valentina Poggi. Giovanna Covi has shared my interest in post-colonial studies, and has inspired fruitful intersections between Caribbean and Scottish literature. (Net-) working for five years in the national research project coordinated by Marina Camboni ("Networking Women: Subjects, Places, Links Europe-America, 1890-1939. Towards a Rewriting of Cultural History") has provided an invaluable source of inspiration and an opportunity to further my research on Catherine Carswell. Additional acknowledgements should be made to my former department — the Dipartimento di Scienze Filologiche e Storiche of the Università di Trento — which funded the greatest part of the work of research on which the present work relies as well as to the Facoltà di Lingue e Letterature Straniere of the Università di Verona which, for the past three years, supported its completion. I also wish to recognise the help that I received from the staff of Edinburgh libraries – the National Library of Scotland, Edinburgh University, the Scottish Poetry Library and the Central – who have always proved highly professional and extremely helpful.

Finally, I wish to thank the several hundreds students who attended my courses in the past fifteen years or so — they proved to be the most sensitive gauge to the interest and the relevance of the subject I have devoted myself to. It is largely through their response that I have persuaded myself that, *yes*, Scottish literature does matter. And not only to Scots.

C. S.
Verona
June 2005

Introduction

Colin Donati

Few nations debate why their literature matters sincethe value and significance attaching to the national character of a 'canon' of works is generally taken as read. Standard practice is to hold appreciation of national provenance in reserve for eulogy as the occasion arises. Why need Scotland be any different? Indeed, to pose the question implied in the title of this volume could be interpreted as silent witness to a doubt.

On the face of it, the Scots have no grounds for cultural insecurity in the matter of literature. Our country has been closely identified with its writers, perhaps more deep-seatedly than is the case with other iconic cultural figures. We possess a literary heritage that ranges back to include, among many other elements, a uniquely expressive and individualised corpus of medieval and renaissance poetry which still has an unusually intimate power to speak to the modern mind. A vigorous, distinctive and nationally heightened literary output was one of the country's most important cultural driving forces in the century just by. And what could be more natural or self-evident than the statement made by Willa Muir, speaking of her 1930s novels in a letter to Neil Gunn, when she writes:

> being Scottish, my approach to any universal problem is bound to be by way of Scottish characters.

So nobody seriously denies that there is a Scottish literature. Yet the premise has not always been routinely assumed to hold.

A dreich critical consensus this time last century held that all prospect of an autonomous national literature in Scotland was dead, effectively smoored oot under the subsuming cultural imperatives of an ascendant and commanding 'British' imperial tradition. Scotland's majority languages of the day – Scots and Gaelic – were deemed to be corrupt and of little relevance in a new gigantist State with 'dominion' over a modern global empire. Most 'native' literary expression was characterised (usually tacitly) as rearguard, parochial and self-limiting – part of a thrawn, vestigial national mettle that would eventually wither on its branch. And such of our canon predating Burns as had *curiously* survived was regarded, if at all, as of interest only to the specialist. Even home-grown critics succumbed to a depressed assumption that incorporation of our writers into a purely 'English' tradition was natural, inevitable and fatal.

With two such profoundly contraposed perceptions within Scotland's critical heritage, it is no surprise that the situation for our literature has been described as a 'predicament'. For better *and* worse, the legacy of this historic dichotomy continues to be felt even into the beginnings of the present devolutionary era. On the one hand, our capital is internationally accorded City of Literature status; on the other, due recognition for that same literature as part of the mainstream in higher education is still, even now, not considered *de rigueur*. At the volatile centre of this dichotomy – as the closely argued and multi-threaded discourse of this timely book invites us to consider – sits the fact of the Union.

Carla Sassi, Professor in the Faculty of Foreign Language and Literature at the University of Verona, takes the challenge contained in this Saltire Society commission very seriously indeed. Our uniquely problematised heritage in her view, gives rise to many singular and (given the right appraisal) positive implications. Where our debate needs to be drawn beyond often ultimately defensive parameters – as in many regards, it still does – then these are precisely the areas that must be unpacked, investigated and elucidated. Professor Sassi does exactly this with the welcome alacrity and acuity of an 'outsider'. Nor does she explore these issues in the domestic context alone. One of the most valuable and important contributions to the debate found in these pages is the compelling and persuasive discussion of these matters in the international domain from an international perspective. Hugh

MacDiarmid once famously avowed his ultimate aim to 'keep Scotland on the main march of the world's interests'. Carla Sassi demonstrates that his ghaist need hae nae worries on that score.

One thing that will not be found in these pages, however, is yet another attempt to reinvent the national canon – a kenspeckle genre of late. In this context that is surely correct. A canonical approach is largely a descriptive one; one that ultimately answers the question what Scottish literature *is*. The question in hand here is why Scottish literature is *important*. Neither the simple fact of its existence nor the quality of its corpus alone can be answer enough. And besides, as Alan Riach suggests in his 1992 introduction to MacDiarmid's *Selected Poems*, it has been hard, historically, to accord Scotland's literature its due canonical status since its 'study', he writes:

> requires a greater degree of contextualization, a more extensive consideration of matters strictly non-literary (and where literary, often comparative) than the honoured and traditional study of canonical texts.

Professor Sassi understands this complexity. Far more importantly, she is positively inspired by the challenge it presents. In this lucid and most deliberately constructed book, she begins to cut and clear – to howk and redd – a few essential paths towards answering that vital challenge. Her methods will not please everybody, but the proof of her success will be in the invaluable ground our debate gains as a result.

This is a narrative that is as much about nation as it is about literature, a self-proclaimed 'work in progress', an attempt to provide a framework that we are free to test out in the areas Professor Sassi does not include. It is an individual passage, a staging post for a new leg in the journey, a tentative proposal for fresh map-reference points. It might even, at times, constitute something of a stripping down and reservicing of parts for the vehicle. There may be unfamiliar sights on the road forward. The inclusion of women writers is not tokenistic, but is integrally and structurally embedded within the argument. Nor does the thesis hang only on a discussion of major figures in our mainstream quality literature; it incorporates a comprehensive reading of the 'secondary' literature as well. Indeed, this is an answer to the question 'why Scottish literature matters' that includes intriguing and relevant discussion of Archibald MacLaren yet nary a mention of the important Scots makar Henryson. Much in this text will surprise, some elements may even vex, but there is no single sentence that does not demand our complete engagement.

If anyone wonders what might drive one of Italy's most respected academics, a clear, dispassionate thinker at the top of her profession, to devote so much of her career in the 'cause' of the literature of a 'marginalised' nation otherwise peripheral in the field of vision of her literary compatriots – and finds herself able to do so, moreover, with such seriousness, optimism, openness, commitment and ultimate maturity of purpose – then all doubt is dispelled in course of these nine contentious, tightly-written chapters. After a full absorption of the arguments, there can be no further mystery.

C.D.
Edinburgh
September 2005

ONE

Approaches and intersections: a view from without

In ways I could not have anticipated, writing about difference brought me a new perception of sameness. I was not after all an island, but a piece of the continent, a part of the main.

Fredelle Bruser Maynard (*Raisins and Almonds*, 1985)

Because this volume, for the first time since this series was designed, has been entrusted to a non-Scottish scholar, it is perhaps appropriate to begin with a few considerations on the perspective from which this vast and extremely challenging subject will be considered, and to set a few necessary limitations — ideological, chronological, and even (inevitably) 'idiosyncratic'. It is crucial to stress, from the very beginning, the problematic nature of the 'object' (literature) under consideration here, and its complex relation to the equally problematic ideas of 'nation' and 'identity': all too often these have been treated as 'natural', and therefore as objective and unquestionable categories. In fact, as we shall see, much (even though not all) of the interest that a journey through several centuries of Scottish literary history yields — to the native as well as to the non-native reader — stems from the complex interaction between these variable terms.

I will then start with a short personal note, pointing out that, because I was not born in Scotland and I do not reside there, there is no immediate, contingent reason why I should claim that "Scottish literature matters"— it is not part of my heritage, nor of my ancestors'. I could therefore simply restrict myself — as many scholars and readers around the world have done before me — to claiming that all (good) literature matters, and that among the writers who, across the centuries, have been recognised as masters, there is a relevant number of Scots. This would be a perfectly legitimate perspective, which would address the 'universal' appeal of many well-known authors, like Scott or Stevenson, by setting them in a wider comparative cultural or super-national context, (e.g. 'Romantic', 'British', 'western', etc.), thus conforming to a practice which has prevailed among scholars until recent times. Conversely, encouraged by the recent, wide-spread tendency towards cultural and political de-centralisation, which has gradually restored dignity to the 'margins', be they 'regions', 'ex-colonies' or — as is the case with Scotland — 'stateless nations', I could narrow my focus to the specificity of Scottish culture (of which literature is a significant expression), to its difference from other cultures, to its uniqueness. However, with no wish to deny the appropriateness of the above approaches, I believe there are further cogent reasons why Scottish literature may be regarded, today, as a valuable heritage beyond the borders of the country where it developed. In fact, like many other scholars in the world, I was drawn to research in this specific field not only by the outstanding accomplishments of its individual writers, by curiosity to explore an 'exotic' culture ("Out of myself and my country I go"[1], as R.L. Stevenson phrased it), to see my personal experience 'projected' onto the screen of a different world in what is regarded as a common cultural 'transference' process, but also because I was intrigued by the animated debate which has surrounded the definition of its history and its canon, and even by the many inevitable and insoluble contradictions that run through it. In short — I was intrigued by what has been described as its 'anomalous' or 'paradoxical' predicament [2]. It is this very 'anomaly', and the consequent difficulty in pigeon-holing Scottish literature according to current critical and cultural parameters, that makes its study a challenging experience, beyond the indisputable interest and value of its multi-faceted and long-standing tradition.

The first of the anomalies concerning the predicament of Scottish culture is perhaps the most obvious, and is somewhat implied in the very title of the present volume, which still betrays the lack of confidence typical of those countries/regions which have been subject to colonisation/marginalisation by a dominant/imperial centre for some time. Everyone would agree that a scholar writing an essay today on, say, 'why English literature matters' or 'why French literature matters', would predictably incur the perplexity of a large part of the reading public, trained, particularly on the 'Old Continent', to believe that national literatures are objects 'out there', clearly defined, which have developed systematically across the centuries, whose status and relevance is not to be questioned. Schools and universities, through curricula designed mostly in the 19th century — that is in the hey-day of the nation-states — have contributed in great measure to the definition of 'great traditions' in terms of a series of separate entities, each characterised by a cumulative unbroken history, and thus by a literature which has been allowed to develop and grow organically. Scotland's history as a nation cannot be referred to this ideal model for several reasons — mainly because Scotland has not been an independent state for three hundred years, and also because it was deprived of its autonomy at the very time (the 18th century) when European nation-states were defining themselves in 'organic' terms. Furthermore, its history is objectively marked by a series of fractures — ethnic, linguistic, religious — which make it extremely difficult, if not altogether impossible, to weave a unitary portrait of the community which inhabits it and of its culture. There have been several attempts at fixing a national unifying myth, especially in the course of the 20th century, but they all led to transient formulations — that is to say even more transient and more fragile than similar identity myths, constructed by nation-states at about the same time. The paradigm of post-Union Scottish culture, as we shall see, is indeed dominated by the notions of fluidity and plurality.

If Scotland is not, quite obviously, a nation-state, it is also difficult to assimilate it fully to the model of a 'minority culture' —

and this can be regarded as the second, and less evident, anomaly. In this respect, it is worth pointing out, even though Scotland, since the Union of Parliaments in 1707, has experienced a process of marginalisation by an unsympathetic central Government, its response to this process seems to have differed substantially from that of many similarly threatened cultures. Here, as we shall see, resistance to cultural assimilation has not led to a desire to set back the hands of time and to revert to a pre-colonial, 'unmixed' past, nor to construct a monolithic definition of Scottishness, shaped on that very model (that of the centralised nation-state) which determined its marginalisation. The illusion of national cohesion, which can be achieved more easily, especially when reinforced by prolonged resistance against a dominant culture, in small countries or regions, has been unattainable in a country like Scotland, 'doomed' to a permanent status of ethnic and linguistic fragmentation. A sign of Scotland's 'anomaly' in this respect, which will certainly strike outsiders, is the fact that while the majority of its inhabitants today would uphold Scots as one of its national languages, they do not speak it currently, unlike what happens, say, in the Basque country or in Catalonia, or even in the Celtophone Highlands. Certainly Scots, in the past ten years or so, has become an increasingly widespread written medium, even in prose and in official documents (the webpage of the Scottish Parliament, for example, is translated into several languages, including Scots), but still today those who write it are not likely to use it as a daily means of communication, while those who speak it (largely the working class and the rural population) are usually unable to write it. A superficial evaluation of this circumstance (and an insufficient knowledge of Scottish history), or a rigid comparison with the model offered by many 'minority cultures', may indeed lead an outsider to rate Scots as a stage language for a stage identity, which, of course, is not the case, as the present study shall make clear.

Furthermore, the lack of a central unifying myth, of a neatly articulated cohesion between the many Scotlands of the past and the present, and the fact that here nationalist movements never promoted terrorism or armed rebellion, as they did in many other parts of the world, have certainly contributed to the 'eclipse' of Scotland's history of antagonism with England and of cultural subordination within the United Kingdom. Of course the erasure of Scotland's specificity was enacted chiefly by British historiography, which conventionally represented the Union as Scotland's step forward into prosperity and modernity. A self-eloquent example of this attitude is that conveyed by Trevelyan's *English Social History* (1942) — a textbook studied by generations of students in Britain as well as abroad:

> For a generation or more the benefits of the Union seemed to hang fire. But after the liquidation of the Jacobite and Highland questions in 1745-46, Scotland sprang forward along the path towards happier days.[3]

Words make the difference — a 'modernised' region, unlike a 'conquered' or a 'colonised' one, does not retain, among other things, an autonomous cultural status. However, if British historians were largely responsible for this questionable interpretation of Scotland's history, it is also true that their perspective was unwittingly corroborated by a wide-spread self-deprecatory attitude on the part of the Scots, who, especially in the course of the 20th century, shared a sense of guilt for being at least partly responsible for their own fate as a 'suppressed' nation. This feeling developed in time into the conviction of not 'being up to one's role' ("The unfortunate thing for Scotland is that it is not an obviously oppressed nation, as Ireland was..."[4], Edwin Muir bitterly remarked) — a conviction which has never been entirely shaken off from Scots' collective conscience.

Finally, there is a third 'anomaly' that should be mentioned, strictly connected to the second. Many critics today raise strong objections to Scotland's predicament being equated to that of an (ex-) colony, understandably so, as it is a status which Scotland can claim only in part: its active and crucial involvement in the building of the British Empire makes it objectively difficult today to include its literature in the so-called post-colonial canon. And yet, undeniably, Scotland has shared with many colonies the painful experience of deterritorialisation and of culture and language erasure (as in the Celtic Highlands) as well as of cultural subordination (enacted, for example, in the degradation of Lowland Scots to a dialect). If the Scots perceived themselves as equal partners, there is no doubt that Dr. Johnson held a very different perspective on their country's position within the Union, as reported by Boswell in the *Journal of a Tour to the Hebrides* (1774): "We have taught you, (said he), and we'll do the same in time to all barbarous nations — to the Cherokees, — and at last to the Ouran-Outangs"[5]. No doubt Johnson's perception was widespread south of the Tweed, and this is just one of the many occasions when Johnson defines Scotland and its inhabitants in strictly colonial terms — the 'barbarians' who have seen at last the (English) light of civilisation. If it is true that Scotland cannot be regarded as an (ex-)colony of the British Empire, it is equally indisputable that there are many self-evident similarities and parallel processes which connect its modern and recent cultural history with this particular status. Anyone familiar with Caribbean or Anglo-African literature, for example, is bound to be aware of themes and strategies which are also distinctive of many post-Union Scottish texts. In this respect, a knowledge of post-colonial theories (which in the past few decades have examined the formation of empire, the impact of colonisation on post-colonial history and culture and the cultural productions of colonised societies) can lead to a challenging re-evaluation of Scottish culture and literature, as well as to a fruitfully broader contextualisation. However we wish to describe the status of Scotland — an internal colony? an ex-colony? a post-colony? a marginalised region? — the notion of 'post-coloniality', in its broader, and by now current, connotation of a critical orientation towards the re-reading of the past[6], is bound to be extremely advantageous. It is undeniable, for example, that also for Scotland — as for many post-colonial cultures — marginality has become "an unprecedented source of creative energy"[7], as the present study aims to demonstrate.

The lack of comparative models for Scottish culture and, consequently, for its literature, has posed serious limitations to its appreciation and discussion beyond its borders and is undoubtedly one of the main reasons for its long-standing isolation. Not an independent state, lacking the cohesion of most minority cultures, covering an ambiguous role between colonised and coloniser, Scotland has found it difficult to define itself in the clear-cut, exclusive terms required by literary critics and cultural historians until recent times. It could be argued that the 'failure' to achieve a unitary, organic definition of its identity has weighed on 20th-century intellectuals as much as other, more obviously adverse historical conditions – in fact, it came to be identified by many Scottish intellectuals with the failure of their culture *tout court*. One of the many bitter expressions of this sense of defeat is articulated by Edwin Muir, in his notorious definition of Sir Walter Scott's country:

> [...] a hiatus, [...] a country, that is to say, which was neither a nation nor a province, and had, instead of a centre, a blank, an Edinburgh, in the middle of it. But this Nothing in which Scott wrote was not merely a spatial one; it was a temporal Nothing as well, dotted with a few disconnected figures arranged at abrupt intervals: Henryson, Dunbar, Allan Ramsay, Burns [...]. [8]

For those who, like Hugh MacDiarmid, had committed themselves to the re-writing of Scotland's cultural history, and were searching for the harmonising threads that would link the Golden Age of its independent past ("Back to Dunbar!", in MacDiarmid's famous slogan) to its subordinated and broken present, this was inadmissible. And yet, there is no doubt that, with the benefit of hindsight, Muir can today be partly rehabilitated. We are well aware, in fact, that by the standards of the 1930s, in a Europe where nations were busy defining themselves in terms of race, of standard language and culture, and where cohesion and purity were quickly becoming synonymous with political and cultural superiority, Scotland's actual lack of a 'centre', and the consequent impossibility of tracing an organic tradition could only be perceived as a fatal flaw. Today we might even regard it as a blessing, in the light of the disastrous outcome of the rise of nationalist movements in the period between the wars, while, from a post-modern perspective, we can easily argue that the fault did not lie so much with Scotland, as with the political/cultural model referred to. Even though we cannot share the pessimism of Muir's critique, today we can certainly appreciate his clear perception of the eccentricity of the Scottish predicament, and the honesty of his statement. By locating his country 'nowhere' and describing it as a hiatus, Muir undoubtedly offered a more pregnant and effective metaphor for Scottishness than many of his colleagues were able to articulate in the same period. The much more popular short lyric by MacDiarmid (or appropriated by MacDiarmid, who challenged Lindsay's initial attribution to Compton Mackenzie [9]), "The Little White Rose", for example, provides us with an undoubtedly poignant and moving image:

> The rose of all the world is not for me.
> I want for my part
> Only the little white rose of Scotland
> That smells sharp and sweet — and breaks the heart.[10]

The few, emotional lines clearly evoke a nostalgia for a (lost) small, whole, 'pure' world which — as a representation of Scotland — seems quite anachronistic and far from adventurous, at least in comparison with other metaphors, elaborated in other poems, namely *A Drunk Man Looks at the Thistle* (1926), where MacDiarmid articulates his most challenging vision by theorising and celebrating Scotland as a 'mongrel' nation, and by revelling in the infinite possibilities offered by the Scots-English language continuum. As we shall see, MacDiarmid partly succeeds in constructing and conveying a positive image of Scotland's plurality of voices ("Scotland small? Our multiform, our infinite Scotland small?"[11]), but the implied 'gap' between the yearning for the idealised and complete "little white rose" and the triumphant vision of a 'mongrel' nation, in fact, articulates the same 'silence' as Muir's hiatus. Both writers, in fact — in their own way — felt the weight of an overarching cultural model and had to come to terms with it. Their first, perhaps imperfect theorisations of Scotland's specificity have great value insofar as they attempt to provide an alternative to the construction of national identity in terms of homogeneity, conceived in the 18th century and dragged on, as we know only too well, to the present day. A stateless nation; a multivocal nation, which expressed itself in three languages (one — Scots — 'creolised' and linked to a second — English — in a continuum); a multiethnic nation, which represented itself in 'regions', could — and would indeed — give the lead in this respect.

Literature, in Scotland as elsewhere, has always been a privileged site for this debate, and has certainly contributed towards the elaboration and the diffusion of new ideas. Furthermore, even a 'conservative' literary text which aims at representing nationhood will tend to do so in a problematic rather than in a prescriptive way, unlike, say, an historical or political treatise. It is not in the nature of a literary text, in fact, to set univocal definitions and to draw definitive borderlines; even when an author purports to portray nationhood according to current definitions, or is animated by a specific ideology, the layered structure of the text will end up problematising and even contradicting his/her original plan. The study of Scottish literature in particular, from 1707 to the present day, will provide the perceptive reader with plenty of examples of this inlaid ambiguity. Darsie, for example, one of the main characters in Scott's *Redgauntlet* (1824), experiences in a very direct and almost physical manner the uncertainty regarding the contours of national identity, when he admires the Solway Firth, a region whose changeable and unpredictable coastline configuration becomes a powerful metaphor for his own predicament:

> [...] I turned my steps toward the sea, or rather the Solway Firth, which here separates the two sister kingdoms, and which lay at about a mile's distance, by a pleasant walk over sandy knolls, covered with short herbage, which you call Links, and we English, Downs. [12]

Darsie, at this stage of the novel, thinks he is English — later on he will discover that he is Scottish. And this is by no means the most shocking of the revelations concerning his family's history he will have to come to terms with. The reader — as in many other novels by Scott, as we shall see — follows him and the other characters in a deeply perturbing and destabilising journey, at the end of which his/her traditional ideas of identity (national, as well as individual) have been definitively undermined. Scott, nominally a supporter of the Union, does much to challenge many entrenched assumptions in this field, and he is only one of many writers who, in the same period in Scotland, do so.

In the past two decades scholars have proved the arbitrariness of the construction of the nation — an immensely powerful creation, which has shaped social life and the organisation of knowledge in modern Europe and a large part of the western world. For Benedict Anderson, for example, a nation is an "imagined political community". It is imagined, he posits, "because the members of even the smallest nations will never know most of their fellow-members, meet them, or even hear of them, yet in the minds of each lives an image of their community."[13] It is not too hazardous to say that this arbitrariness has been a familiar notion and almost a daily experience for Scots in the past three centuries as, after the Union, they were obliged to re-fashion their identity — or re-imagine their nation — in order to fit in the new, composite British state. The adjustments and the conflicts triggered by the adoption of a new supra-national citizenship have deeply affected Scotland and, as happens when things are not easy and straightforward, identity has become an 'obsession' — a healthy one, we may say with the benefit of hindsight, insofar as it has gradually encouraged a more flexible and encompassing approach to issues of identity. In this respect, Scottish literature can provide a valuable model for those countries where still, to this day, national identity is perceived as fixed and unquestionable. The very fact that the Scottish cultural model does not fit the dominant pattern may thus offer — once more — an invaluable vantage point.

Of course, it is one thing to say national identity is an arbitrary construction, quite another to deny its present relevance — something that the present work certainly does not purport to do. Undoubtedly, in its basic idea of a community (albeit 'imagined') with shared values, with a shared memory of its past and its sense of belonging to a territory, the nation still represents a powerful and appealing form of collective identity. The hope (or the ideological orientation) implied in the present work is that such a notion of community may be eventually 'reformed' from a fixed into a permanently problematic category, that is one that may also grant, beside a sense of cohesion and continuity, openness to change and acceptance of the different histories and stand-points of all its members, and that, by defining itself in retrospective terms, may always acknowledge its ever-changing profile.

There is at least one other crucial question that must be addressed in this introductory chapter, one that 'outsiders' are perhaps more bound to ask themselves than natives: is it still necessary to write the present book in 2004, when Scotland has already been given back its Parliament and much of the international recognition it was denied in the past three centuries? Does it make sense, today, to linger on such a 'small-scale' perspective? Certainly the challenge posed by the title of this pamphlet appears less daring today than it did only twenty years ago, when this series was inaugurated by Derrick McClure's introduction to the Scots language, and remarkably less so than in 1936, when the Saltire Society was founded, with the proposed aim to "enrich and foster the cultural heritage" of Scotland's (then) marginalised tradition. In the course of the 20th century, and in particular in the past two decades, Scotland has gone a long way towards a full recognition of its culture, its languages and its literature, and inevitably the defensive attitude, still echoed in the title of the present volume series, has partly lost its momentum. Partly, but not entirely: even though it can be said that the strong compulsion towards the (re-) definition of Scotland's identity and culture against an overarching Englishness belongs to an historical period that is now over, the challenge posed by the Saltire Society in the '30s can be regarded as still topical if invested in a different direction. If the promotion of the study of Scottish culture and literature has involved, until recent times, a struggle to curb Anglicisation and to restore Scotland's sense of a dignified and autonomous tradition, today it might imply a task which is no less exacting — that of checking globalisation and of resisting assimilation to the falsely multicultural, 'united colours' ideal promoted by glossy magazines on one side, and, on the other, the pull towards a closed national model (which seems to be dangerously gaining ground once again), based on exclusivity and intolerance. On the front of globalisation, for example, it seems already rather difficult to curb the interests of the international book-market, or of the tourist industry, which, in their endless search for easy labels to sell their products to an apparently increasingly misinformed public, are largely responsible for the propagation of simplified images of national identity and superficial cultural icons, whose resilience and diffusion seem to defy all earnest attempts to redefine Scottishness. As is the case with the evergreen 19th-century cliché of Scotland as the 'Land of Romance', still exploited in holiday brochures, or with its most recent (symmetrical) reverse, the sub-urban decay of 'Trainspotting-land', not to mention the uproarious and face-painted masculinity of a Braveheart brand of nationalism which has — not too surprisingly — become the favourite icon of an independentist and xenophobic party like the Northern League in Italy. In its attempt to be recognised as a distinctive culture Scotland might find itself — paradoxically — trapped in old and new stereotype definitions. In this sense, writing this book in 2004 can be regarded as still topical and also needed: a re-evaluation of Scotland's distinctiveness might, in fact, provide a valuable alternative cultural model between (or beyond) the two extremes described above.

Finally, a 'cautionary note' is required: one cannot refrain from envisaging risks in too much insistence on dealing with Scottish literature as a separate field of study — a tendency which has developed in the course of the 20th century, as a form of reaction to the marginalisation and the misrepresentation of its tradition. The risks here have to do with a prescriptive turn that literary criticism may, inadvertently, take, or with the narrow applications that it may lead to. Even earnest attempts to re-define Scottishness may result in the creation of rigid categories and thus in the stifling of literary creativity, if definitions are taken as 'dogmas' rather than 'work in progress', as they should be. Scottish literature has certainly suffered immensely from stereotypical approaches: regarded as 'Celtic' from an English perspective (Matthew Arnold, as we shall see, was largely responsible for this), and therefore seen as charged with "an excess of feeling", "fanciful imagination" and a "worship of place"[14], but even mortified by (at times) equally narrow definitions by native intellectuals who wished to redress the balance. This was especially the case at the beginning of the 20th century, when the effort to rewrite the cultural history of the nation led to the marginalisation of writers, literary genres, or works, which were regarded as representative either of an Anglocentric perspective, or of social classes which had given up their Scottishness in order to meet the requirements of the centre. One of the most outstanding victims of this 'revision' was certainly Macpherson/Ossian, along with a host of 19th-century writers, also accused of constructing and propagating the myth of the Land of Romance to meet the literary tastes of English readers. 'Escapist' genres too, like fantasy, were rejected by a generation of intellectuals who, understandably, recognised in realism the only antidote to the (colonial) exoticisation of Scotland.

This 'cautionary note' should extend to enclose a more general statement: a literary text always has a life of its own, behind and beyond its historical and geographical origin, otherwise translations would not be possible at all. Furthermore, as intertextual theory has highlighted, it is located in a 'relational world' — that is, for its meaning it is connected to and dependent on other literary texts, not necessarily organised into tight national/regional compartments. Ideas, words, stories, people travel all the time: no one (luckily) can prevent this, even though many have, in the course of history, refused to acknowledge and record this continuous movement of exchange and crossing. Furthermore, both to write and to read a novel or a poem, or to watch a play, always entails an individual act of interpretation. As literary theoreticians have widely demonstrated, there is never *one* reading, there are as many as there are readers: it is this inherent 'freedom' that defines and distinguishes a literary text — among other things — from other written expressions. To curb it would mean, inevitably, to deny the value of literature.

Having opened this chapter with a personal note, I feel it is appropriate to conclude it in the same fashion. In taking up the challenge of writing the present volume, I feel somewhat encouraged by the awareness that this, at least, is certainly not the first time I have been asked to explain "why Scottish literature matters": in fact it has been almost a daily exercise for the past fifteen years or so. As an academic I have had to explain it to colleagues of sundry nationalities and to face, at times, their scepticism regarding a subject which seemed 'anomalous', and also, as a lecturer, to students, in my own as well as in other countries. If Scottish literature may be regarded today as a reasonably established field of study, even outside its country of origin, when I first started researching in this field, in the late '80s, it was still relatively unexplored, at least 'on the Continent'. I resorted to the critical works then available, mainly written by Scottish scholars and often conforming to a perspective which, quite appropriately, focused on the difference of Scottish culture, especially in relation to England's. I found them immensely stimulating and they certainly opened up new horizons in my studies. In the course of time, however, and especially through teaching, I have been encouraged to look for 'connections' and 'bridges', and to search for useful comparative models in order to communicate my interest to those who knew little or nothing of the historical and cultural background of the writers I was dealing with. The outcome of this research — which can only be regarded as work in progress — is partly contained in the present volume. It is not the final word, something no piece of literary criticism or literary history can ever provide, and it is not a (yet another) 'history of Scottish literature'. More modestly, or more ambitiously, it proposes to explain how the study of Scottish literature can be approached, what makes it valuable, to Scots and non-Scots alike, in short — 'why it matters'. The perspective which informs the present work has been partly highlighted in this introductory chapter — further 'intersections', with issues or theories that I have found useful in my study of Scottish authors will be introduced and annotated along the way. Predictably, there are a series of questions that will be privileged in this 'guided tour' through several centuries of Scottish literary history — these are mainly connected to the representation of national identity in literary texts, and with the relationship between 'centre' and 'margins', or 'coloniser' and 'colonised', a relationship which at times becomes painfully (or dangerously) ambiguous. The same interest in 'margins' has led me to explore the contribution of those Scots who have been misrepresented or ruled out *tout court* in literary histories until recent times: women writers in particular, but also representatives of 'minorities' which, for different reasons, have not been regarded as part of the native community — 'invisible Scots', as they have been named. In adopting this particular perspective I have certainly been encouraged by the work of those Scottish scholars who, before me, have dealt with the same or a similar approach — among these, the writings of Angus Calder, Cairns Craig, Robert Crawford, Alan Riach, Roderick Watson and Christopher Whyte have provided an invaluable source of inspiration.

As far as the selection of the texts discussed is concerned, consistently with the ideological line expounded above, I have opted for maximum inclusiveness: I have cited from canonical and non-canonical texts alike, I have considered established writers as well as virtually unknown ones, and I have also made reference to journals, diaries and letters, thus siding with those critics who regard them as a 'private' literary genre, with its own set conventions and limited audience. Because the intersection between 'nation' and 'literature' is obviously privileged in the present volume, I have also felt justified in referring, occasionally, to historical, philosophical or political texts. As, regrettably, I do not speak any Gaelic, I have necessarily resorted to the available English translations of the original literary texts and at times, to the assistance of Gaelic-speaking friends. Finally, I wish to stress that the choice of authors and texts discussed in the following chapters cannot be regarded in the least as exhaustive — as my predecessors in this series know well, 1,500 years or so of Scottish literary history will never fit in a slim volume like this. I have chosen, therefore, what I regarded as the most pertinent and useful examples in my line of argumentation, and I have not felt compelled to cite an author just because s/he is deemed a 'classic' — with much regret for all those I was forced to leave out, among whom I could number some of my favourite writers, as well as friends. Hopefully, seeing that they are in very good company, they will not be offended.

The quotation chosen as an epigraph to the present chapter also testifies to what has been my scholarly journey through (and beyond) Scottish literature. It is, in fact, by writing about (Scottish) difference, that I have learnt to discern sameness. In fact, as Homi Bhabha has explained:

> . . . it is by living on the borderline of history and language, on the limits of race and gender, that we are in a position to translate the differences between them into a kind of solidarity.[15]

References

1   Quoted in R.L. Stevenson, "Personal Experience and Review", in R.L. Stevenson, *The Amateur Emigrant/ The Silverado Squatters*, London: William Heinemann, 1925, Vol.16, p.65.

2   See for example Cairns Craig, "Constituting Scotland", in *Irish Review*, No.28, 2001, pp. 1-27.

3   G.M. Trevelyan, *English Social History. A Survey of Six Centuries. Chaucer to Queen Victoria*, Harmondsworth: Penguin, 1967, p.432.

4   Edwin Muir, *Scottish Journey*, London: Heinemann & Gollancz, 1935, p.29.

5   *Johnson's Journey to the Western Islands of Scotland and Boswell's Journal of a Tour to the Hebrides with Samuel Johnson*, R.W. Chapman (ed.), Oxford: Oxford University Press, 1970, p.72.

6   David Theo Goldberg, Ato Quayson (eds.), *Relocating Postcoloniality*, London: Blackwell, 2002, p.14.

7   Bill Ashcroft, Gareth Griffiths, Helen Tiffin, *The Empire Writes Back. Theory and Practice in Post-Colonial Literatures*, London: Routledge, 1989, p.12.

8   Edwin Muir, *Scott and Scotland*, London: George Routledge, 1936, pp.2-3.

9   The poem had originally been published anonymously in *The Modern Scot*, July 1931, and erroneously attributed to Compton Mackenzie in Maurice Lindsay's anthology — *Modern Scottish Poetry*, 1976. At MacDiarmid's insistence the poem was successively credited to him.

10   Hugh MacDiarmid, "The Little White Rose", in *The Complete Poems of Hugh MacDiarmid*. Vol.I, Michael Grieve, W.R. Aitken (eds.), Harmondsworth: Penguin, 1985, p.461.

11   Hugh MacDiarmid, "Direadh I", in *The Complete Poems of Hugh MacDiarmid*. Vol.II, Michael Grieve, W.R. Aitken (eds.), Harmondsworth: Penguin, 1985, p.1170.

12   Walter Scott, *Redgauntlet*, Oxford: Oxford University Press, 1985, p.31.

13   Benedict Anderson, *Imagined Communities*, New York: New Left Books, 1991, p.6.

14   The phrases in inverted commas are from an article which appeared in the TLS in 1938: Doris N. Dalglish, "Towards a Nationalist Literature. The Scottish Renaissance", in *Times Literary Supplement (Special Section. 'Scottish Literature Today')*, 30th April, 1938, p.x.

15   Homi K. Bhabha, "Dissemination. Time, Narrative and the Margins of the Modern Nation", in Homi Bhabha (ed.), *The Location of Culture*, London: Routledge, 1994, p.170.

TWO

Once upon a time there was a kingdom…
Scotlands of the past

To be sure, only a redeemed mankind receives the fullness of its past — which is to say, only for a redeemed mankind has its past become citable in all its moments.

Walter Benjamin ("Theses on the Philosophy of History", 1955)

The ambitious aim of the present chapter is to present an overview of pre-Union Scottish literature — not so much with the intent of covering effectively such an extended period of time, but rather with that of highlighting a few methodological problems which arise when we try to define a 'national' literature, and in particular one (like Scotland's) which has been marginalised by a dominant culture for a long time. The vastness and the heterogeneity of such a period undoubtedly defy any attempt at generalisation, nonetheless, given that the Union of 1707 marks a watershed in Scotland's literary and cultural history, it is wise to use it here as a *terminus post quem*. In Europe, as is well-known, the 18th century marks the birth of the modern nation-state, the establishment of capitalism and the rise of imperialism. Ideals of ethnic and linguistic homogeneity of the national community are gradually introduced and deeply affect its dynamics as well as the relation between the writer and his/her readers — literature becomes a 'national' artefact, defined in terms of standard language and of conformity to precise cultural tenets. If 'modernity' leads to a rigid codification of social and ethnic relations along 'universal' and 'objective' lines, and to the demarcation of national boundaries as 'natural' and therefore fixed (as well as necessary to protect its inhabitants from outside vexations), then 'pre-modernity', in its lack of systematisation, undoubtedly allows for a higher degree of fluidity in taxonomic matters. Incidentally, the dramatic shift into the modern age takes on an extra connotation in Scotland, as it coincides with its de-nationalisation, *de facto*, even though not *de iure*. That Scotland becomes a stateless nation at a time when the nation-state establishes itself as the political ideal model in Europe partly accounts, as we shall see, for the complexity of this country's cultural history.

Where does Scotland's literary history start from? This is no secondary question, as most readers will be certainly aware. Setting a starting point, in fact, also means setting a firm perspective on our subject matter. A survey of the numerous histories of Scottish literature that have been written from the late 19th century to the present day will easily confirm this. Representations of the past are always, in large measure, influenced by our present (as Sir Walter Scott knew well, long before New Historicism theorised it), so points of departure and arrival have also varied considerably in the course of a hundred years or so. The setting of a starting point, in our case, will depend, first of all on how we wish to define 'Scotland' — politically or geographically, from an ethnic/cultural and/or a linguistic point of view. It will of course depend also on how we define the term 'literature' — as a corpus of written texts, as the term etymologically implies, or stretched to include also verbal art performances (characteristic of oral cultures); 'high', that is relative only to works regarded as superior by aesthetic and artistic standards, as opposed to 'low', that is inclusive of popular or daily forms of expression; articulated in the traditionally established genres, such as epic, drama, lyric, novel, etc., or enunciated in hybridised forms, such as the ballad, story-telling, or concrete poetry.

Defining these common and apparently neutral terms entails, then, an ideological act with important implications for our study, and one which will in turn influence the kind of questions we may wish to ask. The 'where do we start from' issue is, then, particularly critical when we deal (as we are going to do in the present chapter) with the origins of a national literature. It is, in fact, in the most ancient and vague recesses of time, often fading into the realm of legend, that the myth of the nation has found its richest nourishment. As theorists have highlighted in recent times, nations are 'imagined communities' and "like narratives, [they] lose their origins in the myths of time and only fully realise their horizon in the mind's eye"[1]. There is, therefore, a high degree of arbitrariness and ephemerality in any construction of nationhood and, as a consequence, there is also an inherent complicity between 'nation and narration'. A nation is not a 'natural' and therefore fixed object; rather it can be described as a symbolic force creating cohesion within a given, and inevitably heterogeneous, community. It is through the 'narration' of itself that such a community achieves that cohesion, albeit transitorily. The 'narration of the nation' will never be a finite product, for the precise reason that it will be influenced by cultural and political changes, as well as by the variations in the extent and in the composition of the community that — across the centuries — 'imagines' itself. Some of the myths or 'traditions' that make up a national identity can prove particularly resilient, others are much younger than most of the members of a given community will ever suspect — rarely do they survive the span of two or three generations. What theorists have brought to light, in what is an ongoing debate, started in the 1980s, beside the fundamentally arbitrary nature of ideas of nationhood, is the leading role that literature plays in their construction — not surprisingly, as a literary text can weave fact and fiction, legend and history in a much more effective and persuasive way than other modes of expression. Writers have articulated representations of nationhood either in response to the establishment's desires or requests (the practice of patronage, for example, often encouraged the production of eulogistic/patriotic texts throughout the medieval and Renaissance periods), or spontaneously, as an individual commentary on traumatic or extraordinary socio-political events (many historical novels represent a case in point). In both cases, however — as we shall see — the literary text is bound, by its very polysemic nature, to problematise or to subvert even the most conservative projects of political propaganda. In this sense literature represents a fundamental source for both the historian and the literary critic — the former cannot ignore the power and resilience of literary constructions of nationhood, the latter has to be aware of the social/political mechanisms underlying such forms of collective identity when s/he is faced with the task of dealing with a national literature.

While it is unquestionable that recent theoretical inquiries represent an invaluable contribution to our understanding of western history and culture, it is also undeniable that, by challenging the authenticity of the nation, they have indirectly put into question its *raison d'être*. In fact, according to many theorists today (both in the field of geopolitics and in that of literary/cultural studies) the nation has become an entirely superseded organisational model, and is bound to decline or even disappear in the 21st century, as the world, today, is already largely functioning at a supranational and infranational level. [2] This may be bad news for those stateless nations — like Scotland — which have been denied for centuries political and/or cultural independence, and which (re-)enter History at this inauspicious moment. It is obvious that for a community which has passed through a ruthless process of marginalisation and inferiorisation, the question of national identity cannot by all means be dismissed as anachronistic and superseded. It is equally obvious that — for the same reason — the definition of national identity as an 'arbitrary' construction can be easily accepted by a metropolitan intellectual, but can sound very menacing to a minority or a marginalised group, which might envisage in these theories a new and subtler form of discrimination.

One of the points that the present study wishes to make, in fact, is that the idea of nation is still — unquestionably — crucially relevant in today's world, and deeply ingrained in western culture and imagination. This is not to say that it will always be so, but rather that, at present, the symbolic force of this form of group identity is still powerful and that, given its persistence, it is possibly wiser to retain it, pragmatically, and to strive to *rethink* it, rather than deny it altogether. On this perilous journey, between the contemporary Scylla and Charybdis of extreme localisms/resurgent revanchisms and overwhelming globalisation, the eccentric experience of a stateless nation like Scotland can prove an invaluable contribution towards this much needed redefinition.

Where do we start from, then? Language, along with ethnicity, has often played a major role in the definition of nationhood, frequently leading to markedly 'exclusive' perspectives. Literary historians who belonged to, or identified with, the Scots-speaking part of the country frequently recognised in Barbour's *The Bruce* (the earliest surviving poem in that language, written between 1320-1395) the first Scottish literary landmark. It is noteworthy that the same text, incidentally, also gives shape to one of the founding epics and most enduring myths of the Scottish nation. Others, acknowledging the older age of the Celtic heritage, set the 'beginning' in the 11th century with the *Duan Albanach*, a poem of twenty-seven verses, providing a list of the kings of Scotland from its legendary origins to the time of Malcolm III. As far as the Gaelic tradition is concerned, discriminating between 'Irish' and 'Scottish' (or 'invader' and 'native') is obviously difficult at this stage — given the chronological distance of the period considered and the consequent difficulty of reconstructing it exhaustively, and the fact that the cultivated forms of the languages largely coincided for a very long time (the so-called Classical period of Gaelic literature — both Scottish and Irish — extended from the 12th to the 17th century). Yet, this poem — in all probability produced by an Irish-born author — refers to and draws from local history, beside being written in a language which would, in the course of time, develop into one of modern Scotland's languages. Another well-known poem, the *Gododdin* (ca. 600 AD), incidentally also the most ancient extant literary text in Great Britain, was written in a language which subsequently disappeared in North Britain (Brett — a Celtic-P variety — which survived in south-west Scotland at least as far as the 11th century [3]) has very often been expunged from Scottish literary chronologies, notwithstanding the fact that it relates the feats of a tribe of Britons who lived between the Forth and the Tyne, whose chief was Lord of Din-Eidìn (later Dunedin and then Edinburgh [4]) and that — as is generally accepted by scholars — it was produced in North Britain. That literature in Scots has often been considered as the mainstream of the Scottish tradition, and literature in Celtic as a 'sideline', is hardly surprising, if we consider that the former has represented, for several centuries, the dominant ethnic group. Scottish universities in the 20th century, even though committed to the promotion of scholarly interest in native cultures, have, paradoxically, sanctioned this hegemonic relation by designing different curricula — 'Scottish' and 'Celtic' — thus discouraging, until recent times, an inclusive and comparative approach to the literatures of Scotland.

The problem of an 'exclusive' outlook arises even more manifestly whenever the discussion of Scottish literature becomes subordinated to the urge to identify the first 'nucleus' of the Scottish nation, and to trace a smooth, linear progression, connecting the remotest past to the present day. Again, the options can vary — the first embryo of the Scottish nation could be identified, as it has often been the case, with the establishment of the capital in Edinburgh by the Canmore dynasty, or with the ascent to the throne by King Robert the Bruce. But how useful is this historical/political perspective when we deal with literature? Isn't it perhaps going to affect the way we select and discuss individual 'Scottish' texts? Aren't we going to exclude, in this way, texts written, say, in Orkney or in Shetland, which were not part of this first nucleus of the Scottish nation? Or works written in languages and by ethnic groups that did not subsequently develop into the Scottish tradition, as we know it today? Such questions get complicated by another issue, that of the definition of 'literature' in ages so distant from our present. Can the carved symbols and inscriptions of the Pictish stones, or the Roman writing-tablets of Vindolanda be considered as part of Scotland's literary heritage? Can we treat the Middle Ages chroniclers as 'fabulators', and thus consider historical records written in Latin, or in Old Norse, like the 13th-century *Orkneyinga Saga*, as part of Scottish literature too? When we deal with the 'literature of the origins', in Scotland as elsewhere, the physical filter set by history is already very rigorous — while many sources were lost, others were marginalised, when not deliberately destroyed, by dominant ethnic groups or political/religious authorities/factions in power at different times. Obviously, while problems related to the transmission of texts are bound also to characterise more recent historical periods than the one taken into consideration here, the issue becomes much more relevant when we deal with a distant past. In this case, therefore, a 'retrospective' and extensively inclusive outlook will not only prove beneficial but essential.

We can then stretch (retrospectively) the field of 'Scottish literature' to include all the texts produced in the territories comprised in present-day Scotland; in this way we will perhaps sacrifice those teleological 'lines of continuity' that literary historians of the nation have often been keen on setting (in Scotland as elsewhere), but we will certainly produce a picture of a layered past that is more likely to reflect the complexity of our present. Certainly the King's famous directive to the White Rabbit — "Begin at the beginning and go on till you come to the end: then stop" — is not very useful when you deal with literature. There is never *one* beginning in literary histories — something begins, of course, and that is the (written) documentation of a certain language. But the fact that even that is only a conventional beginning should be always borne in mind.

We will therefore start drawing our map of ancient literary Scotland, symbolically, with the first carved Pictish stones — the 'silent' texts inscribed on the land, whose presence has been acknowledged and even revered by the inhabitants of Northern Britain throughout the centuries, and whose symbols have haunted the imagination of generations of Scottish writers. As it is obviously the archaeologist's task (and not the literary historian's) to decode their language and to reconstruct the context in which they were engraved, we will limit ourselves to considering how the 'enigma' of the Picts has often attracted, in the past two centuries or so, the interest of scholars as well as of amateurs who, on the basis of scanty documentation, have not hesitated to formulate conjectures regarding their origins and language. The Picts have become — *malgré leurs* — a powerful national literary myth: in the eyes of many modern Scots they ended up representing the Scottish 'proto-nation' — ethnically homogeneous, 'native' and non Indo-European, and therefore non Germanic and non Celtic [5]. This perspective was certainly attractive for those who, in given historical periods (especially at the close of the 19th century and in the first decades of the 20th), regarded the 'celticity' of Scotland as an undesirable trait — either because they regarded the Scottish Gaels as embarrassingly 'primitive', or because they perceived the Irish immigrants as a threat to the integrity of their national community. As the fog of history gradually lifted from this ancient people, it was ascertained that they had indeed represented a distinct political and cultural entity until the second half of the 9th century, that they had occupied a wide territory which included Eastern and Northern Scotland, the Outer Hebrides and the Northern Isles, and that, on the basis of the little evidence available, they had spoken a Celtic-P language and written in two alphabets (Latin and ogam, the latter in all probability adapted from the Irish ogam). Eventually, they had adopted the language of the later settlers — the Scots. The adoption of a language different than the native one does not necessarily entail — as we know today — the disappearance of a people's culture (are the Scots or the Irish 'English' just because they speak English?), so we can presume that Pictish culture did survive as a distinct expression for a certain period, and that to a certain extent it crossed with that of the Scots, to develop into something else.

Scotland was also inhabited by peoples who did not necessarily come to stay, or who immigrated and settled taking with them their language and customs — as happens today. It is not out of place to record, then, on our literary map of the origins, also the voice of the invaders/settlers who garrisoned the wall that Hadrian had ordered to be built between the Solway Firth and the River Tyne in order to separate Romans from 'Barbarians', south from north. The Romans who lived in Vindolanda between 85 AD and 130 AD distinguished themselves as a literate community, which included the officers' wives, possibly their children, and the slaves who attended them; in all probability they had an articulate social life, as the numerous writing-tablets, unearthed in this particular area, partly testify. A fragment brings to life a glimpse of an intimate dialogue between two ladies, obviously bound by a deep friendship:

> *Claudia Severa to her Lepidina greetings. On 11 September, sister, for the day of the celebration of my birthday, I give you a warm invitation to make sure that you come to us, to make our day more enjoyable for me by your arrival, if you are present (?). Give my greetings to your Cerialis. May Aelius and my little son send him (?) their greetings. I shall expect you, sister. Farewell, sister, my dearest soul, as I hope to prosper, and hail.* [6]

The writing-tablets of Vindolanda, beside offering a fascinating *tranche-de-vie* portrait of the life of the Northern British Roman community, can be regarded (with some flexibility), just like letters or journals today, as literary documents — a private genre, with a limited audience. It might be then a little questionable, but not outright unacceptable, to include them in our 'literary map of the origins'. Incidentally, the writing-tablets include at least one fragment which is unquestionably literary, that is a line from Virgil's *Aeneid* — "interea pavidam volitans pinnata per urbem" ("Meantime winged Rumour, flitting over the shaken encampment"[7]) — possibly the writing exercise of a child in the family of a commanding officer.[8]

The Romans withdrew from Britannia at the beginning of the 5th century. Their impact was possibly irrelevant in ethnic terms — even though recent studies have brought to light a more consistent interaction with native peoples than has been traditionally recognised by scholars. The ruins of their cities, forts, monuments remained long after their departure. Latin inscriptions have represented more 'silent' texts inscribed on the Scottish landscape, which were to raise fantastic conjectures, especially after the Union of 1707, when scholars and writers often projected onto the stage of the ancient world the fate of the modern Scottish nation, like Sir John Clerk of Penicuik (1676-1755), who recognised in the mightiness of the Roman defensive walls the valour of the antagonists (the Caledonians) against whom they had been built.

The Romans' most lasting heritage, however, the Latin language, spread in Britain and throughout Europe, not so much as a consequence of the Roman military conquest, but through the diffusion of Christianity. Latin becomes the language of texts of religious instruction and inspiration first, and the *lingua franca* of secular scholars later. It would be the medium of instruction in Scottish universities until the 18th century. If we wish to consider the lives of the saints as the forerunners of modern fiction, then the first Scottish 'novel' was written in Latin: *Vita Sancti Columbae* (*The Life of St. Columba*) was written by an Irish monk Adomnan (the ninth abbot of Iona and successor to Columba), in the 8th century, and describes the life in the community of Iona. Besides providing essential information on the monastery and its close links with Ireland and western Scotland in this period, it also provides a charming evocation of 'our island', as it is often referred to, and of the different places the saint visited in his Scottish peregrinations — Skye, Islay, Tiree, Mull, Loch Ness, are just a few of the many place-names that the contemporary reader will instantly identify as a familiar 'geography' of Scotland. Perhaps the most vivid glimpse of the monks' life on Iona is represented by the evocation of how visitors to the island often announced their arrival:

> Quadam Dominica die ultra saepe memoratum clamatum est fretum. Quem audiens Sanctus clamorem, ad fratres qui ibidem inerant, 'Ite,' ait, 'celeriter, peregrinosque de longinqua venientes regione ad nos ocius adducite.' [9]

> *One Sunday there came a shout across the Sound. Hearing it, St. Columba said to the brethren who were with him: 'Go quickly and bring at once to us the pilgrims who have arrived from a far-away district.'* [10]

The map of literary Scotland between the 6th and the 9th century is then marked by a plurality of ethnic groups — it includes Scots, Picts, Britons, Norsemen, and Angles. Languages spoken and written in this period (and well into the 11th century) include Gaelic, Brittonic, Old Norse, Latin and Old Northumbrian, with three alphabets in use — Roman, ogam and runic. The borderline between 'invaders' and 'natives' is certainly elusive at this stage, similarly, it is not easy to define the individual contributions of the various ethnic groups to the shaping of the 'Scotland' to be, or to reconstruct their interaction and exchanges. Some of the early intersections between languages and peoples are, however, recorded: at least two Pictish monuments are inscribed with both Roman and ogam alphabets [11], and one of the best-known and most outstanding monuments of ancient Christianity, the 8th-century Ruthwell Cross (produced in the same region where it now stands — Dumfriesshire) exhibits the poem "The Dream of The Rood", engraved in runic characters and adapted to Old Northumbrian, as well as quotations from the Old and New Testament in Latin. An act of the General Assembly of the Kirk of Scotland of 1642 decreed that the cross be thrown down and shattered, a fate followed by other testimonies of pre-Reformation Christianity, regarded as equally idolatrous. At that time many valuable sources (including in all probability Pictish ones) were also destroyed. Fortunately, the fragments of the cross were not lost and they were retrieved and re-assembled in 1802, thanks to the personal endeavour of the minister of the same church where it had been cast down 160 years before [12]. The "Dream of the Rood" is today regarded as one of the masterpieces of Anglo-Saxon literature — its most famous MS copy is today preserved in the *Vercelli Book*. The Ruthwell poem, however, represents a Northumbrian adaptation, or variation of the original version, and does not coincide perfectly with it:

Ruthwell: Krist wæs on rodi. Hweþræ þer fusæ fêarran kwomu æppile til anum: ic þæt al bihêald

Vercelli: Crist wæs on rode hwæðere þær fuse feorran cwoman to þam
æðelinge ic þæt eall beheold

Christ was on the Cross. But hastening nobles came together there from afar. I beheld
it all [13]

The runic alphabet was a Germanic invention — it was used by
Anglo-Saxons and continental tribes and, with very few variations,
also by the Norsemen who raided and settled in north-eastern
Scotland and in the Northern and Western isles, starting from the
8th century. In 'Scandinavian' Scotland archaeologists have brought
to light numerous objects dating back to the so-called 'Viking
period' (ca. 800-1050), inscribed — after the Germanic fashion —
with the name of their owner. Runes often appear side by side with
Pictish or Irish decorations and symbols, in the typical syncreticity[14]
which characterised this age and these territories. The inscriptions
are always very short — minimalist texts indeed, which can be
regarded as evidence of literacy, not necessarily of literariness.
However, once more, we feel allowed to stretch our boundaries of
'literature' and to include them in our map of the origins. After all,
the man who wrote "Gautr reist rúnar" (*Gautr wrote the runes*) on
the steatite whorl spindle found at Westness, Rousay, Orkney [15]
seemed concerned — if the anachronistic reading may be allowed
in this context — with claiming 'authorship' as much as 'ownership'.

The Norsemen's contribution to the linguistic and cultural
configuration of Scotland is certainly substantial and it extends
well into our present: Orkney and Shetland still today boast a
literary tradition in languages/dialects which retain many features
of the Norse language, while the oral literature of Gaelic Scotland
has preserved a remarkable body of heroic ballads and legends
related to the Vikings. Some of the works produced in these regions
have travelled well beyond their native borders: the 13th-century
Orkneyinga Saga is regarded by scholars as one of the masterpieces
of medieval Germanic literature — a classic, which testifies to the
existence of what has been described as a 'Northern
Commonwealth'. Once more, as with the Picts, the Norse 'sidelined'

identity was the object of a lively debate in modern Scotland, especially at a time (between the end of the 19th century and the 1930s) when Scottishness started being redefined against an overarching Englishness. Even though traditionally portrayed negatively, mainly as adventurers and looters, Vikings provided then a comfortable Germanic alternative identity, which on one side granted distinctiveness within a predominantly 'Anglo-Saxon' British nation, and on the other satisfied those who did not identify with the Celtic heritage of Scotland.[16] In the course of the 20th-century 'Viking' characters haunted the imagination of quite a few novelists – regarded by some as a war-mongering and bloodthirsty people and as the disreputable ancestors of the worse aspects of modern Scotland, as in James Leslie Mitchell's *Lost Trumpet* (1932), they were portrayed by others as ruthless adventurers, and yet also capable of bravery and stoicism at sea, as in Neil Gunn's *The Silver Darlings* (1941), or in Eric Linklater's *The Men of Ness* (1932). Others, like George Mackay Brown (a native of Orkney) in his *Greenvoe* (1972), have committed themselves to continuing the tradition of the 'chronicler of the islands', who impersonally relates – in the style of the anonymous author-narrator of the *Orkneyinga Saga* – the story of his community.

The 11th century marked, with the increasing influence of the Normans, the addition of yet another language – (Norman) French – to the spectrum of idioms already in use in Scotland. If French, spoken mainly by the Norman noblemen, or by their entourage, never became the language of the peoples who inhabited the regions under their direct rule in England, this was even less the case in southern and eastern Scotland, where the actual presence of settlers was minimal. However, the Normans' political and administrative system of reforms – along whose lines the kingdom of Malcolm Canmore and Margaret, and then of David I, was to develop – and hence their cultural impact on the country, was profound. Besides French, the Normans contributed to the spread of Latin as the secular language of administration, thus encouraging crossings and intersections with two extremely rich European literary traditions.

It is worthwhile remembering that one of the most celebrated queens of Scotland, the 'English' Margaret, spoke French, as well as the southern dialect. She also inspired a text of great literary charm, the *Vita Sanctae Margaritae*, written in Latin by her (Anglo-Norman) confessor — Turgot, bishop of St. Andrews. A definitely secular testimony of the Norman influence on Scotland, which lasted over a century, is represented by the Arthurian romance *Fergus of Galloway*, written towards the end of the 12th century, or the beginning of the 13th, by a Frenchman, Guillaume le Clerc, who, in all probability, had lived in this part of Scotland for some time. The place-names mentioned in *Fergus* can still be found on the map of southern Scotland, as in the following passage, which traces the flight of the white stag chased by Perceval:

> La contrée de Landinore/ Trespassa outre sans arest,/Si s'en entra en la forest/De Glascou qui molt estoit grande./ Onques em bos, n'em pré, n'en lande/ Ne fist li cers arestement;/ En Auroie vint erraument,/ Illeuc — les illes sunt;/ N'a plus beles en tout le mont.[17]

> *Without pausing it passes through the whole Lammermuir district before entering the very extensive Forest of Glasgow. The stag never halted in any woodland, meadow or heath, but sped on to Ayr, the home of the fair women, than whom none are more beautiful in all the world.*[18]

Literature in Middle Scots, like that in Middle English, is characterised by a significant bond with the Old French tradition. The status of French as a language of social and cultural prestige was, in fact, further reinforced through the 1295 'Auld Alliance' — a military agreement between France and Scotland, which lost its power only after the Union of Parliaments and the Jacobite Rebellions. French was also the idiom in which one of Scotland's most powerful and controversial icons expressed herself with most ease. Mary Queen of Scots — born in Scotland but brought up and educated at the French court — was a learned and refined lady, who spoke, besides French and English, also Latin, Greek, Spanish and Italian. Her poems, in French, were highly praised by Pierre de Ronsard, her life-long friend and mentor: it is only recently, however, that they have been collected and translated into English. She was the object of endless representations, within and without Scotland, either very discrediting and articulated from a misogynist and/or anti-Catholic stance, as exemplified by John Knox's notorious appeal "Against the Monstrous Regiment of Women" (1558), or extremely romanticised, as in many 19th-century paintings, depicting a languid heroine with all the appealing sensuousness of the sacrificial victim and none of the real-life weight of an historical character. Mary Stuart is but one of the many queens or regents neglected by a historiography clearly little prone to investigate the role of female rulers, in Britain as well as in Europe. Her delicate rhyming verses represent a stunning and touching journal of her short life. Besides any evaluation of her political role as a sovereign of the Scottish nation, it is surprising that her literary voice has been silenced for such a long time:

> Comme autres fois la renommée
> Ne vole plus par l'univers
> Ici borne son cours divers
> La chose d'elle plus aimée.

> *My fame, unlike in former days,*
> *No longer flies from coast to coast.*
> *And what confines her wandering ways?*
> *— The very thing she loves* [19]

In the period under consideration, however, it is undoubtedly Gaelic literature that represents the oldest and richest continuing Scottish tradition, both written and oral. Classical Gaelic was used from the 12th till the 17th century, when the Scottish vernacular, that had gradually distinguished itself from Irish, supplanted it. It must be a sorrowful experience, for members of the contemporary community, to discover how scanty a treatment is reserved for this flourishing period of their cultural history in most surveys of Scottish literature: the gap, in fact, reflects not only the gradual sidelining of this tradition, following the Unions of Crowns and Parliaments and the establishment of the Anglo-Scottish supremacy, but also the vast destruction of manuscripts in this language which took place before the age of antiquarianism. Certainly, if this devastation had not occurred, it would have been possibly more difficult for Dr. Johnson and his followers to 'prove' the inferiority of a tradition on the grounds of its being mainly 'oral'. The marginalisation that followed the labelling of Celtic culture as 'primitive' — an evaluation shared by the English and the 'Lowlanders' alike — did not succeed in extinguishing it, but certainly went a long way to curb its diffusion and development in the modern age.

The period between 1375 and 1707 is characterised, as R.D.S. Jack has recently phrased it, by a "polymathic linguistic tradition"[20] — which means not only that texts could be written in at least four different languages (Scots, Gaelic, English and Latin as well as Norman French and Old Norse), but also that, as the linguistic boundaries shifted, contact and exchange were quite common, as witnessed in the 16th-century trilingual manuscript *The Book of the Dean of Lismore*. The same goes for translations. In order to represent effectively the map of literary Scotland at this stage, a 'web' is certainly a more useful model than the traditional 'branching tree' — rather than a pattern of mainstreams and sidelines, a network of 'links' (as in the internet), variable, expanding, open, can account more effectively for the fluid, multi-directional relations between texts, authors, across language and political barriers. It is, in fact, quite obvious, that the different communities — largely defined by the language in use — overlapped and intersected and often transcended national boundaries: Latin connected Scotland to the rest of Britain and Ireland in the early period, to France and Europe in the Middle Ages and beyond; Gaelic bound it to Ireland; Anglo-Norman to England, France and the many European regions which had come under Norman rule; (Old) Norse to the Scandinavian countries. While it would be obviously incorrect to state that this 'polyedricity' is unique to Scotland, it is certainly true that cultural and linguistic plurality has remained, in the course of centuries, a specially distinctive mark of this country, which, for diverse historical reasons, has never been able to smooth difference into one 'core', consistent national identity.

There is at least one other question, which we should address in this chapter, namely Scotland's troubled relations with England. It is well known that, in the course of the centuries, following the Norman conquest, the south-north divide, both in linguistic and cultural terms, became gradually more evident, with the south progressively gaining more power and more prestige and boasting primacy over the 'backward' northern regions. One of the first and most famous utterances of the southerners' sense of advantage is, significantly, linguistic, and is contained in John of Trevisa's 14th-century Middle English translation of the Latin *Polychronicon*. The translator, who employs the Midlands dialect (which would develop into modern English), makes fun of the northern variety (spoken in Yorkshire and stemming from Northumbrian, the Old English dialect from which both modern northern English dialects and Scots originated), describing it scathingly as "scharp, slytting and frotyng, and unschape". Not only was it cacophonous and 'shapeless', but it was also unintelligible: "We Southeron men may that longage unnethe undurstonde", the author lamented. This is hardly surprising: the inferiority of the 'Other', in fact, has often been assessed first on linguistic grounds: in Attic Greek, for example, *barbaros* described derogatively a foreigner as someone whose speech was unintelligible — 'stammering' (as suggested by the onomatopoeic root of the word). In a similar way, Irish Gaelic was perceived as a 'gabble', a de-humanised form of expression, by English colonisers in the Elizabethan age, as testified by Miranda's words to Caliban, the archetypical colonial subject ("I . . . Took pains to make thee speak, taught thee each hour/ One thing or other: when thou didst not, savage,/ Know thine own meaning, but wouldst gabble like/ A thing most brutish"[21]). It is ironical perhaps, but certainly not strange, that the first king of Scotland and England sanctioned the north-south divide in clearly hegemonic terms: James VI, in his treatise on *Daemonologie* (1597), written six years before the Union of Crowns, explains that remote northern countries ("such wild partes of the worlde, as Lap-land, and Fin-land, or in our North Iles of Orknay and Schet-land") are more subject to the lures of witchcraft, on the grounds that : ". . . where the Deuill findes greatest ignorance and barbaritie, there assayles he grosseliest, as I gaue you the reason wherefore there was moe Witches of women kinde nor men."[22] After the Union of Parliaments, rescuing northern Britain from the dismal coarseness of its language and culture would be one of the Scottish Enlightenment's declared missions.

That the relation between England and Scotland was one of (almost) permanent conflict was a fact well known to many Europeans. Dante, for example, depicts them in his *Divina Commedia* with a hint of contempt — both haughty and mad in their being in perpetual conflict with one another, and thus bound to face God's wrath on Doomsday:

> *There will be seen the pride which makes men thirsty*
> *And sends the Scot and the Englishmen quite mad*
> *So that they cannot stay within their frontiers*

(Paradise XIX, 121-23) [23]

Given the extent and the intensity of the tension between the two countries, it was perhaps inevitable that Scottish nationhood should have shaped itself (as was the case with many other European countries) also through conflict with and resistance to its meddlesome neighbour. However, it is also true that the political history of a nation does not account entirely for its cultural production. To accept this equation would lead, in fact, to a *reductio* — a contraction of the value and the scope of a tradition which was always, as the present chapter has maintained, in rich and complex engagement with other cultures. Besides, it is also questionable that the construction of national identity should be seen as dependent only or mainly on defensive strategies. A recent strain in Scottish fiction and film — represented by two popular movies like *Rob Roy* and *Braveheart*, both incidentally appearing in 1996 — has stressed, in a dangerously simplified and polarised manner, the relation of conflict and difference between England and Scotland. It is of course alarming that, at the dawn of the 21st century, such an archaic model of self-definition should still cling to our imagination, and that Scotland's cultural identity should be represented principally in terms of its 'resistance' to England.

Much has been said — in the course of the 20th century — about the forced anglicisation of Scotland following the Reformation (and the circulation of the English Bible) and the Union of Crowns. While these events certainly favoured — on a political level — the successive Union of Parliaments and Scotland's loss of independence, on a strictly cultural level it is worthwhile to acknowledge that the spread of the English language in itself can hardly be regarded as a negative thing. It was the successive inferiorisation of the native languages which was damaging and not at all a 'natural' consequence of the diffusion of English. Many scholars today would agree that it is a romantic (or 'essentialist') notion that a cultural identity can only be articulated in *one* (native) language. Languages can be appropriated by their speakers and bent to tell different realities — the story of the English language, today spoken in hundreds of different varieties around the world, provides a very eloquent example of this. As far as Scotland is concerned, diglossia (or even polyglossia) was obviously a condition common to many of its educated citizens in the course of the period here taken into consideration (and also well beyond it) — it is dubious that they expressed their national identity only through one privileged, linguistic medium. In this sense, English is no less 'Scottish' than Scots or Gaelic.

A full re-evaluation of the networks of *reciprocal* making which inextricably bind Scotland and England, culturally and linguistically, long denied (from entirely different perspectives) by both parties, is probably what is most needed today. The interchange between the two countries — always strong in pre-Union times — accelerates considerably after 1707.

References

1 Homi K. Bhabha, "Introduction", in Homi K. Bhabha (ed.), *Nation and Narration*, London: Routledge, 1990, p.1.

2 See E.J. Hobsbawm, *Nations and Nationalism since 1780. Programme, Myth, Reality*, Cambridge: Cambridge University Press, 1992 (2nd edition), pp.191-192.

3 Matthew P. MacDiarmid, "Brett and Pict, Taliesin and Aneirin in Early Scotland", in Steven R. Mc Kenna (ed.), *Selected Essays on Scottish Language and Literature*, Lewiston/Queenston/Lampeter: The Edwin Melle Press, 1992, pp.1-12.

4 John T. Koch (ed.), *The Gododdin of Aneirin. Text and Context from Dark-Age North Britain*, Cardiff: University of Wales Press, 1997, p xiii.

5 Katherine Forsyth, *Language in Pictland. The Case against non-Indo-European Pictish*, Utrecht: de Keltische Draak, 1997.

6 The letter is from Claudia Severa to Sulpicia Lepidina, both wives of *praefecti*, stationed at Vindolanda between 97 AD and 103 AD. Translation from: Alan K. Bowman and J. David Thomas, *The Vindolanda Writing-tablets. (Tabulae Vindolanenses II)*, London: The British Museum, 1994, p.257.

7 Virgil, *Aeneid*, Oxford: Oxford University Press, 1986, Book 9, Line 473, p.267. Translation by C. Day Lewis.

8 Alan K. Bowman and J. David Thomas, *The Vindolanda Writing-tablets. (Tabulae Vindolanenses II)*, London: The British Museum, 1994, pp.65-66.

9 *Adamnani Vita S. Columbae*, (ed. J.T. Fowler), Oxford: Clarendon Press, 1920, Lib. I, Cap.32, p.109.

10 Adomnàn of Iona, *Life of St. Columba*, (edited and translated by Richard Sharpe), Harmondsworth: Penguin, 1995, p.135.

11 Katherine Forsyth, "Literacy in Pictland", in Huw Pryce (ed.), *Literacy in Medieval Celtic Societies*, Cambridge: Cambridge University Press, 1998, p.44.

12 David Howlett, "Inscriptions and Design of the Ruthwell Cross", in Brendan Cassidy (ed.), *The Ruthwell Cross. Papers from the Colloquium Sponsored by the Index of Christian Art, Princeton University, 8th December 1989*, Princeton, N.J.: Princeton University, 1992, p.71.

13 From the West side of the Cross. Transcription and translation from ibid., p.85 and p.88.

14 Following an established practice among post-colonial critics I have used the term 'syncreticity'to describe "the process by which previously distinct linguistic categories and, by extension, cultural formations, merge into a single new form." (See Bill Ashcroft, Gareth Griffiths, Helen Tiffin, *The Empire Writes Back. Theory and Practice in Post-Colonial Literatures*, London: Routledge, 1989, p.15.)

15 James Graham-Campbell, Colleen E. Batey, *Vikings in Scotland. An Archaeological Survey.* Edinburgh: Edinburgh Press, 1998, p.42.

16 Julian D'Arcy, *Scottish Skalds and Sagamen. Old Norse Influence on Modern Scottish Literature*, East Linton: Tuckwell Press, 1996, pp.37-52.

17 *Le Roman des aventures de Fregus*, Francisque Michel (ed), Edinburgh: Abbotsford Club, 1842, pp.7-8. This version is based on the MS held at the Bibliothèque Nationale, Paris.

18 Guillame le Clerc, *Fergus of Galloway. Knight of King Arthur*, (translated and edited by D.D.R. Owen), London: Dent, 1991, p.4.

19 Mary Queen of Scots, *Bittersweet Within My Heart. The Collected Poems of Mary, Queen of Scots*, (translated and edited by Robin Bell), London: Pavilion Books, 1992, p.86-87.

20 R.D.S. Jack, "Critical Introduction", in *The Mercat Anthology of Early Scottish Literature. 1375-1707*, R.D.S. Jack, P.A.T. Rozendaal (eds.), Edinburgh: Mercat Press, 1997, p.xxx.

21 William Shakespeare, *The Tempest*, Act I, Scene II, 415-19.

22 King James, VI of Scotland and I of England, *Daemonologie*, Book III, Chap.III, London: Bodley Head, 1922-1926, p.70.

23 Dante, *The Divine Comedy*, (translated by C.H. Sisson), Oxford: Oxford University Press, 1998, p.435.

THREE

Dislocations and relocations: writing in the 18th century

In time his coming among them became another tale they told and he would listen to it with a kind of wonder, as if what they were recounting had happened ages ago, in a time beyond all memory, and to someone else.

David Malouf (*Remembering Babylon*, 1994)

The Union of Parliaments marks a dramatic turning point in the social and political life of Scotland: not only does it usher the country into modernity and into the imperial enterprise, but it brutally drags it out of History. For the world, Scotland ceases to exist as an autonomous political entity to be gradually absorbed, nominally, by England. By the 19th century this process is complete and it becomes absolutely normal for Europeans to refer to its writers and inhabitants as 'British' or, more often, as 'English'. 'Scottishness' is gradually adjusted to coincide with England's *alter ego* — a new identity altogether, to whose construction British (Scottish as well as English) writers contribute between the 18th and the 19th century. Romantic landscapes, the empty vastness of the moors inhabited by the echoes of Ossian's sad ghosts, a lost, glorious and picturesque past, are but some of the staple ingredients that form the newly tailored 'exotic' representation of 'Northern Britain', which gradually spreads in Europe and in the world. Scotland, no longer an independent state, does of course retain a strong sense of cultural distinctiveness, but the selective (and biased) mediation of London makes it almost impossible to perceive this beyond British borders. What the Union originates, then, among other things, is a long-term short-circuit in the communication with the 'outside world', generating a painful gap between the internal fabrication of national identity, and its external perception — a discontinuity which has not yet been entirely healed, as we shall see, in the present day. It is, however, this very discontinuity that triggers in Scotland a unique and wide-ranging meditation on (national) identity, which still today represents perhaps one of the most distinctive features of Scottish culture and literature.

The Union was narrated by generations of British historians as an act of free will on the part of Scotland, which had gained prosperity and stability by leaving behind political division and 'primitive' ways of life. The spontaneous protest of the people, who strongly objected to an Act they had not been called to approve, was first silenced in the streets and then in history books. Much later, in the early 20th century, deep disillusionment with the politics of the central government along with the economic depression eventually gave impulse to a drastic re-reading of these triumphant historical fictions, at least on the part of the Scots: the Union was then seen as Scotland's unforgivable act of submission to its long-term neighbouring rival and as an irredeemable divorce from its past — a political suicide that had dried up the national imagination and had led to a pervasive cultural stasis. The restoration of the Scottish Parliament in 1999, following the 1997 Referendum, removed the 1707 Act to a somewhat 'safe' distance, thus making it more manageable and open to a more balanced assessment, especially as regards to its far-ranging cultural implications. In fact, there is certainly some truth in both the above (extreme) perspectives: the Union with England undoubtedly hindered many areas of Scottish life and it provoked much discontent in many of its subjects, but it is equally undeniable that even north of the Tweed it was saluted by some with enthusiasm and that it did open up the country to new possibilities. That this crucial and much debated historical event can now be re-considered in its complexity and problematicity is certainly essential not only to historians but also to literary scholars.

Among the consequences of the Union, it is perhaps more relevant to the present study to stress that it triggered off a pervasive, collective 'act of imagination' on the part of the Scots. In fact, whether by an act of free will or by coercion, consciously or unwittingly, they had to re-define themselves anew as a stateless nation within a new, nationless state. Even for the staunchest of the unionists this involved a sequence of acrobatics: re-defining the idea of Scottishness; moulding a new British identity; balancing the two into some poised synthesis. Harmony is not an altogether easy achievement in this context, and the whole century is run through by contradictory impulses: on one side the effort to resist dissolving into the new super-state by articulating the distinctiveness of Scotland's history and heritage (an act of 'survival' which — in these terms — had never been necessary before), on the other, a massive endeavour to conform to southern standards and to gain ascendancy in the newly-born Union. In the age of the rise of the nation-state and of the politics of state centralisation, Scotland is then marked by an eccentric and isolated experience: while other independent states gradually harmonise themselves into a national image characterised by unity and homogeneity, Scotland is confronted by the insurmountable reality of heterogeneity, within its borders as well as within 'Britain'. No doubt this complex negotiation of the terms of her identity is also a source of great anxiety, in an age dominated by monolithic beliefs, but it is also, unquestionably, among the primary sources of the stunning wealth of 18th-century Scottish literature, in Scots, Gaelic or English. This is, incidentally, also a time of fruitful intersections among literary traditions, across linguistic barriers, as we shall see. Contrary to what one may think (and to what the 'Scottish Renaissance' writers theorised at a later stage), the 'submission' of Scotland boosts, for a long period, its cultural and literary production.

Even though Scotland has, at times, been referred to, like Ireland, as an 'internal colony', what takes place after 1707 cannot be reduced easily to the black-and-white opposition between coloniser-colonised (a dichotomy whose epistemological validity has, at any rate, been partly challenged by recent criticism[1]). It is a much more complex dialectic — one characterised by a wide spectrum of relations and negotiations between the two cultures, and which, in the end, alters permanently not only the idea of Scottishness, but (even though this has never been properly acknowledged) also that of Englishness. To deal with this complexity is not easy, and one of the problems with which Scottish literary historians have been faced in the 20th century is that of finding an adequate interpretative model for describing it. The fact that the term 'unique' has often been (and still is) used to convey the problematic cultural stance of this country testifies to this difficulty. 'Uniqueness' has often been — in this context — a synonym for isolation.

Even though Scotland was not a 'colony' in the most common sense of the word, it is the interpretative model offered today by (post-)colonial cultures, which can account for its problematic predicament, its multifaceted and even contradictory realities. In particular, the experience of 'dislocation', that is the physical as well as the cultural and linguistic displacement inflicted by foreign invasion or settlement, which marks the life of the colonised, also distinguishes post-Union Scotland. Migration, forced or voluntary, within or outside Scotland, displaces Highlanders from their native land, while the gradual erasure of their culture and language in favour of Anglo-Scottish replacements permanently alters the contours of what is 'home' for those who remain. The Lowlands also undergo a similar process of alienation, even though the forces at play here are (partly) endogenous — cultural dislocation, in this case, is more often the outcome of a spontaneous will to conform to 'English' values. It is unquestionable, however, that even those who enthusiastically support the Union, do experience different degrees of cultural denigration, and have to renegotiate their role within the new United Kingdom. Optimism and faith in the possibility of a positive renewal of Scotland's predicament may prevail in the Age of Improvement, but the toll to be paid — in psychological terms — will soon become manifest, even to those social classes which have promoted and supported the Union.

The imperial joint venture with England then, paradoxically, leads Scotland to share with its colonies a very similar experience of marginalisation, while, on the other hand, it establishes it among the leading imperial powers of the western world.

Another fruitful way to account for post-Union Scotland's problematic stance is that of referring to those theories of the nation which have brought to light how a community tends to give itself an ethnic/linguistic identity *against* a foreign and threatening group — national identity would then be defined mainly through an *us* vs. *them* 'defensive' pattern. If, up to 1707, Scotland, through its long history of conflict with England, had partly constructed its identity against its aggressive and menacing neighbour, the Union undermined this very pattern by introducing a national supra-identity which blurred, at least superficially, such demarcated boundaries. The Union was — as we know very well — promoted by an élite, which did not need, at that time, public ratification for its implementation, and whose main motivation was economic.[2] The unconditional support for the Union was guaranteed, in the following two centuries, by those social classes which most benefited from the new political order. The 'spontaneity' of the decision, albeit taken by a minority, and the fact that most of the leading intellectuals did not raise their voice against the Union, made it impossible for subsequent generations to say "we are the victims" — the cohesion implied in the simple use of this pronoun was not possible in Scotland in the same way as in other colonised countries. The imaginary line that separates *us/them* was not 'national', but rather ran along class and ethnic divisions and could not be traced with reassuring ease. As we shall see, it is this very impossibility of cohesion, foregrounded in historical and political contingencies, that marks Scotland's peculiar formulation of national identity in the modern age.

The most significant and dramatic outcome of the Union is undoubtedly the outburst of civil war in Scotland. The Jacobite rebellions have been often reassuringly represented — in popular and romanticised versions — as a mainly English/Scottish conflict; in fact, if a simplification is possible, the conflict was — in Marxist terms — between those who clung to the native social and economic system, and those who espoused the cause of 'modernisation' and, consequently, of the anglicisation of Scotland already started with the Union of Crowns. The frontline ran mainly, then, between the Gaelic Scots of the Highlands and the anglicised Lowlands. The struggle had also class and religious connotations — the Catholics (Scottish as well as English), who supported the Stuarts' cause, were successively either stigmatised or exoticised (e.g. in Walter Scott's novels), following the fate common to losers, while the lower classes were more brutally affected by the defeat than the landed aristocracy. Factions — as is often the case — cut across national boundaries, in a way that made all successive simplifications of this corner of Scottish history, at least problematic. Once more, the *us/them* line appeared hopelessly blurred.

Out of this dark conflict — developing at the very heart of the Enlightenment — at least one clear certainty emerged, the definitive banning of Celtic culture from Britain and the beginning of the forced anglicisation of the Highlands. The Empire struck here more methodically and 'scientifically' than England had done in Wales four hundred years before: it was not simply a matter of territorial conquest, so much as of cultural annihilation. This was implemented through draconian laws which made native cultural and linguistic expression illegal, and through strategies of humiliation and denigration of the Gael's heritage and way of life. Yet, the extreme forms of physical, social and individual dislocation suffered by the Gaels, like those (often much harsher) suffered by extra-European colonised people in the age of imperialism, became also the source of creative energy and of an unprecedented cultural and literary renewal. It is possibly within this cultural and linguistic area that some of the most extraordinary literary texts of this century were in fact produced.

Few writers epitomise the predicament of the Gaelic Scottish writer in the 18th century more adequately than James Macpherson, born in 1736 in Badenoch, a region which was the epicentre of both the first and the second Jacobite rebellion. While his *Poems* testify to the Gaels' odyssey in this historical period (the reference to civil war in the Latin epigraph from Lucan to his *Fragments of Ancient Poetry* is eloquent in this respect), the extraordinarily unequal fortune of his work provides a striking example of the divorce between 'internal' and 'external' views of Scotland, which has been mentioned at the beginning of this chapter. James Macpherson's work can only be fully appreciated through an understanding of his predicament as a Gaelic writer adjusting to a changed political context, which now openly aimed at the erasure of his native culture. As recent criticism has revealed, it is no mere chance that — while he was immensely popular and influential in Europe — he was ostracised in life and, after his death, utterly marginalised in Britain on strictly 'moral' grounds, as the accusation of producing a literary hoax, a text which was not 'authentic', originally mounted by Johnson, eventually prevailed over aesthetic considerations. In his later years he gave up literature in favour of historical writing, but even as an historiographer he managed to attract criticism and stir the indignant response of scholars (this time Irish), when he 'demonstrated' — in his ambitious *Introduction to the History of Great Britain and Ireland* (1771) — that the Scottish Celts were an autochthonous ethnic group. It cannot pass unnoticed today that in this way Macpherson severed his native culture's roots from 'mother' Ireland, thus turning it into the most ancient and noblest of British native cultures ("Such are the inhabitants of the mountains of Scotland . . . Their language is pure and original, and their manners are those of an antient and unmixed race of men."[3]). As many intellectuals of his time, he did not question the goodness of the Union with England, rather he committed himself to the negotiation of a space for the Celts in the new British nation. Both his literary and historical writings aimed at proving his ancestors' valour and dignity in the face of the conquering Anglo-Saxons, and thus at attaining that equality *within* heterogeneity that the new regime was promoting only in words.

The issues of 'authenticity' and 'historical truth' are of course quite beside the point in this context: Macpherson's texts are located on "the borderline of history and language" [4] and they represent a point of conflict and intersection between cultures (Gaelic/English), between past and present, between codes (oral/ written). He is necessarily ambivalent, as he inhabits the space 'between' cultures — a space of encounter, translation and 'transculturation'. Macpherson's 'forgery' provides, in contemporary critical terms, a novel fabrication of the past — an attempt to reconstitute his people's history in an acceptable literate form, and within the dominant literary discourse. His Ossian, then, today can be described as a re-writing in a ('Doric') style, meant to meet the aesthetic tenets of Enlightenment Aberdeen, where Macpherson had attended the University, and where he had discovered that Homer, born in a 'primitive' society, had written poetry that was superior to that of the more civilised Attic age. In this light, the indication that the poems were contained in an original manuscript can only be seen as instrumental to their validation as 'literary texts' in a changed cultural context, where the written word prevailed over the oral.

Macpherson's narrative was fiercely contested by Johnson, whose line of argumentation was at least as objectionable — on factual grounds — as his interlocutor's, given his utter ignorance of the Gaelic language and culture. Johnson's attack was, first and foremost, aimed at discrediting Gaelic culture through the 'incontrovertible' deduction that, as the ancient manuscripts mentioned by Macpherson did not exist, then, by extension, no written literary tradition existed in the Highlands. Johnson's logic pinpoints a series of 'binary oppositions' — written vs. oral, primitive vs. civilised, authenticity vs. forgery — which stand for the difference between the two cultures, while firmly subordinating the second to the first. In the typical binary logic of imperial discourse (which was to be applied systematically to extra-European cultures by British colonisers) heterogeneity is re-structured in hegemonic relations. The Anglo-Saxon (written) tradition is then established as the norm, while the Celtic (oral) culture represents a marginal form of expression — 'rude' and 'unpolished', as implied in the word *provincial*, according to the definition provided by Dr. Johnson's *Dictionary*.

The ossianic *querelle*, in Britain, then, focuses not so much on the aesthetic value of the *Poems*, as on the mode of transmission and on the authenticity of the text — a projection of the more crucial battle for the definition of the hegemonic relations among ethnic groups within the new British nation. Britons, at this early stage, can only represent themselves as a mixed people, marked by a "genetic *concordia discors*", a harmony in diversity, where the roles for the component parts that make up the whole are preserved and fixed, as Weinbrot has highlighted in his study: "Celtic imagination, Anglo-Saxon liberty, Classical Roman constraint, together with Christian and Hebrew contexts and spirituality. . .".[5] Cleansed of its subversive message, Macpherson's Celtic Ossian will be easily 'tamed' to occupy one of these predefined 'slots', thus becoming a powerful instrument in the creation of the illusion of an harmonious unity within diversity, to the extent that, in the 20th century, his 'British Celts' will be perceived by Scottish intellectuals as a sign of submission and consequently expunged from the emergent national literary canon. European readers, entirely unaware of the political and cultural stake in this confrontation, simply enjoyed *The Poems of Ossian* as a powerful and modern literary creation: the *Poems* were appropriated by innumerable writers and artists, 'translated' into several other languages, moulded into new stories and images. Possibly, they recognised and appreciated the 'modernity' of Macpherson's work better than their British contemporaries — the bare and godless landscape, the disembodied voices, the 'unfinishedness', the minimalist and dry language, the pervasive melancholy of a text like *Fragments of Ancient Poetry* did indeed represent an innovative literary language. It is also possible that they were attracted by the liminality of Ossian's heroes, suspended, as they are, between past and present, between cultures and languages — a liminality which made them unsettling and 'subversive' at home, but also more apt at speaking across borders than categorical representatives of the 'centre' like Johnson. Little surprise, then, that today Macpherson can be described as one of the most 'international' of the Scottish (and British) writers of this century — boasting a continuous success which extended for over one hundred years.

By deciding to write in English Macpherson had chosen — among other things — 'visibility' beyond Scottish and British borders, that is the possibility to reach a vast reading public. He had also chosen to write his poems within the British/European literary conventions of the time, which made only a few stylistic concessions to the rich oral tradition he liberally drew from. The fate of those who did keep writing in their native language and within the established rhetorical and stylistic modes of the Celtic Classical tradition, challenging the severe restrictions imposed on the expression of Gaelic culture by the central government, was inevitably one of isolation and oblivion — it was unlikely that their fame reached Edinburgh, let alone the literary circles in London. And yet, in the words of all Celtic studies scholars, this is a period of great literary creativity and experimentation in written verse. The dismantling of the traditional Highland social organisation inevitably leads Gaels to intensify the contacts with Lowland cultural institutions — many of the upper classes attend the Scottish universities, or become part of the urban intelligentsia. English and Latin literature become increasingly familiar to educated Gaels, who are now inspired to introduce new themes, new metrical forms and a new diction in the otherwise conservative classical Celtic tradition. In the Highlands, in the 18th century creative writing in the native tongue undergoes an expansion rather than a contraction (possibly because language remains the only licit form of cultural expression), with Gaelic now being used also in prose, and in its modern, spoken varieties. The reaction is not as some may expect, given the context of cultural inferiorisation, one of withdrawal or closure, on the contrary, it shows a strong impulse towards resistance, identified in renewal rather than in the attempt to retrieve or preserving 'purity'. Names like Alasdair Mac Mhaighstir Alasdair (Alexander MacDonald), Iain Mhic Fhearchair (John

MacCodrum), Rob Donn MacAoidh (Robert Mackay), Dùghall Bochanan (Duguld Buchanan), Uilleam Ros (William Ross), Donnchadh Bàn Mac an t-Saoir (Duncan Bàn), are still largely unknown to the world. As Ronald Black reminds us: "while the work of Milton (1608-74) first went under the glass of scrutiny in 1645, that of Ian Lom (c.1625-post 1707) had to wait until 1964"[6]. In fact, it is not before the second half of the 20th century that most of these writers appear in translation, and thus reach (at least potentially) the English reading public. Until then, they are largely regarded as an 'anthropological' phenomenon — outside any 'line of continuity' in European or world literature.

The Union intensifies cross-cultural exchanges and 'hybridisations', which, in fact, had taken place even in the centuries before, between Highlands and Lowlands. Scottishness is re-negotiated not just within the British nation, but also between Gaels and 'Anglo-Saxon' Scots, as the Union indirectly requires that Scotland should shape a new, consistent national identity. It is not a negotiation between equals though, as southern Scots speak from a politically stronger stance: while Highlanders are obliged to learn the English language, Lowlanders are not compelled, either by law or by uncoded prejudice, to learn Gaelic. Predictably, the idea of Scottishness which takes shape in this century is moulded solidly on Anglo-Scots culture. The Gaels, as far as the 18th century debate is concerned, are 'erased' from Britain, and relegated to the status of Scotland's primitive 'Other'. In the 19th century, as we shall see, certain aspects of their culture will be appropriated by the Lowlands and woven into the new (imperial) vision of Scotland.

In a ground-breaking study of 1988, Simpson has described 18th-century Scottish literature as being marked by "multiplicity of voice, fragmentation of personality, and the projection of self-images" which "recur with a frequency and intensity that are quite remarkable"[7]. Scottish writers develop a 'Protean' identity, according to Simpson — ever shifting and multi-faceted. He also points out how this peculiarity has often been used against Scottish writers — one of the many instances of how lack of organicity or cohesion (essential to English standards) has been interpreted as a handicap or a 'fault'. Interestingly, other terms or phrases used by literary critics in reference to this century — like 'paradox', 'dualism', 'crisis of identity' — all basically convey an idea of eccentricity with respect to the 'norm', represented and promoted by England and, more generally, a growing sense of imperfection and inadequacy. A paradigmatic case is certainly that represented by Robert Burns — an extremely articulate and challenging author, who achieved immense popularity in Edinburgh as well as in London. He partook of the literary taste of the period, writing polished epistles and satires in impeccable Augustan style, but he also continued the popular tradition of Scottish songs and ballads; he wrote in English as well as in Scots — more often he shifted subtly from one idiom to the other, exploiting the whole 'creole' continuum that still today links the two kin languages, anticipating, in many ways, the experimentation of 20th-century Scottish writers. Unlike other Scottish writers of the same period, who can be more easily assimilated to an 'English' model, Burns is markedly 'different', and his difference is undoubtedly unsettling — not so much because he deals with Scottish themes and settings in a Scottish language (a literary practice that dates back well before the Union), but because he is able to shift and combine both worlds. Like Macpherson, Burns inhabits and voices the space between the binary oppositions into which 18th-century culture was organising the world: country/city, vernacular/language, Scottish/English, primitive/civilised. Hugh MacDiarmid, over a century later, will reformulate this predicament in a self-conscious and militant manner (for which his 18th century fellow countrymen lacked yet the ideological instruments), as the *locus* "whaur extremes meet" and his selected 'home'.

It is the ambivalence of Burns combined with his wide-spread popularity, that becomes subversive for the centre. The main concern of English critics will be that of relegating him to the safety of a purely 'Scottish' dimension — locally relevant, and therefore (almost forgivably) eccentric by English standards, as epitomised in Matthew Arnold's notorious contemptuous assessment of the poet (and, by extension, of all Scottish literature and culture), written in 1880, in the hey-day of the Empire:

> The real Burns is of course in his Scotch poems. Let us boldly say that of much of this poetry, a poetry dealing perpetually with Scotch drink, Scotch religion, and Scotch manners, a Scotchman's estimate is apt to be personal. A Scotchman is used to this world of Scotch drink, Scotch religion, and Scotch manners; he has a tenderness for it; he meets his poet half way.[8]

It is necessary to remember that the status of 'eccentric' was first bestowed on Burns by a contemporary and a fellow countryman — Henry Mackenzie, who, in his pleading for a due recognition of the Bard's achievement, had no choice but to set him against the yardstick of the English canon. The humble tone of his words, however, betrays a strong pride in the poet's work — while he concedes that Burns' literary achievements cannot be compared to Shakespeare's, he actually goes a long way to suggest that such likening is conceivable:

> Though I am very far from meaning to compare our rustic bard to Shakespeare, yet whoever will read his lighter and more humorous poems [...] will perceive with what uncommon penetration and sagacity this Heaven-taught ploughman, from his humble and unlettered station, has looked upon men and manners.[9]

Mackenzie's somewhat clumsy 'rescue' of Burns in terms of a 'heavenly' exception to the 'rule' that sees the Scottish (vernacular) poet as an unlettered peasant, several steps below the English Bard, could of course be taken as an instance of that 'self-stereotyping' attitude later denounced by the Scottish Renaissance intellectuals, stemming from an acquiescent submission to England's supposed cultural superiority. The creator of the "Man of Feeling" was, in fact, articulating a typical Enlightenment stance. Scottish philosophers in particular had focussed their speculation on the 'stages' of civilisation and on what they saw as a linear progression towards 'improvement' conceding, however, that primitive societies

— given their greater capacity to express emotion freely and genuinely — could achieve a higher form of poetry than the more civilised ones. While the Enlightenment vision of a progressive history of society provided the European fledgling empires with the most formidable ideological alibi for the colonisation of reputedly inferior civilisations (the "white man's burden", in Kipling's words) in the 18th and 19th century, it also shaped the ideological tools with which the margins were to 'resist' the centre. In Mackenzie's apology for Burns (as in Macpherson's defence of his *Ossian*) we can, therefore, identify, along with an 'act of conformity', also a cryptic 'line of resistance' against the English cultural primacy, as well as an attempt to appropriate the dominant discourse in order to assert the value of his native culture. His (superficial) acceptance of the norm represented by the centre is, in fact, characteristic of colonised cultures, as witnessed by the middle class 'Ascendancy' in 19th-century Ireland, or the "class of persons Indian in blood and colour, but English in tastes, opinions, in morals, and in intellect", who Macaulay despised and yet thought beneficial to the proper functioning of the Empire in India.[10] Yet, this apparently submissive attitude, traditionally despised and dismissed by independentist or nationalist groups in many post-colonial countries as an 'aping' of the 'masters', has been revalued in its ambivalent and hence disruptive nature. Homi Bhabha has termed this process 'mimicry', and has highlighted how this mimetic attitude works like a cracked mirror: the colonised, on whom the coloniser's standards have been imposed, cannot but reproduce the 'norm' imperfectly, reflecting back to the centre a deformed image of the model s/he wishes to conform to.[11] The Irish and the Indian subjects who imitate the English will never become like them — they will be mocked, because of their accent or manners, and yet the very imperfection of their imitation carries the seeds of the failure of the colonial authority. In this light, even Mackenzie's apparently humble 'act of conformity' conveys a challenge to the centralised configuration of the English canon, and Arnold's firm refusal to grant Burns citizenship within it is eloquent not simply of the literary tastes of the period, but also of the deep unease which the poet's 'hybridity' inspires.

As contended before, the relation between margins and centre involves a complex network of negotiations, which cannot be summarised conveniently in a 'black and white' opposition, and which, as argued by Bhabha, entails acts of appropriation and compromises in both directions. The process of negotiation over relations of power between England and Scotland is still reasonably fluid in the 18th century, in the aftermath of the Union, but it will gradually crystallise in the 19th century — as exemplified by Arnold's acrimonious judgement — into the familiar stereotypes which still linger in descriptions of Scotland's languages and culture.

What about women writers in the 18th century? Historians, until recent times, have often omitted to specify that the vast majority of women were illiterate, even though not necessarily unlettered. In Scotland, as elsewhere in Europe, their education was regarded as at best unnecessary, at worst dangerous. It is worthwhile to remember that the consequences of this widespread fear of women's 'knowledge' (and of their power) had already reached its climax in the persecution of witches (the vast majority of whom were female) in the 17th century — a persecution which, at least in Britain, had its ideological foundation, incidentally, in the treatise on *Daemonologie*, written in 1597 by James VI of Scotland, later I of England, as mentioned in the previous chapter. It is interesting to witness how in James' three dialogues the bias against the 'primitive' North overlaps with gender prejudice — evidence of how closely interwoven constructions of national/ethnic and gender identity always are.

The last witch to be executed in Scotland (a woman accused of taking part, with her daughter, in a coven) was burnt in Dornoch in 1727, when Adam Smith — one of the 'fathers' of modernity — was just a four-year old boy. If, by the time Smith had grown into a young man, the age of superstition was rapidly waning before the 'light' of reason, it is also true that the appeal to universality and rationality of the Enlightenment philosophers did not significantly alter women's subjugated role in society. Witches were not to be burnt on public squares any longer, but the fears and prejudices which had led to the persecution of so many women were still there. Rousseau, in *Emile* (1762), attacked social injustices, with one notable exception — he explained that men and women are made for each other, but their mutual dependence is not equal:

> *Woman is made up to give way to man and to put up with even injustice from him. You will never reduce young boys to the same condition, their inner feelings rise in revolt against injustice; nature has not fitted them to put up with it.*[12]

Scottish philosophers did not think differently: Adam Smith, in his *Wealth of Nations* (1776), simply erased contemporary women's engagement in labour outside the home (which was substantial, as recent studies have highlighted) and described work as a 'male preserve'.[13] More in general, both Hume and Smith contributed to the promotion of a gender-based organisation of society and labour, with men concentrating on 'production' and women destined to 'reproduction'. Incidentally, Hume also tackled the issue of female chastity, substantially corroborating the ancient and well-rooted male fears of a female free sexuality, which had also been the main concern of the standard book on witchcraft — the 1486 *Malleus Maleficarum* ("The Hammer of Witches") — a source of inspiration for both Catholics and Protestants. Hume's approach to women's 'natural' inclination to lust is decidedly more amiable, but the prejudice is still all there:

> As to the obligations which the male sex lie under, with regard to chastity, we may observe, that according to the general notions of the world, they bear nearly the same proportion to the obligations of women, as the obligations of the law of nations do to those of the law of nature. 'Tis contrary to the interest of civil society that men shou'd have an entire liberty of indulging their appetites in venereal enjoyment: But as this interest is weaker than in the case of the female sex, the moral obligation, arising from it, must be proportionably weaker. And to prove this we need only appeal to the practice and sentiments of all nations and ages.[14]

It should also be remembered, in this context, that the much-praised (and justly so) Scottish Parish school system which, in the

18th and 19th century allowed young children of the poor classes to access education, did not, in fact, extend to include girls. In a recent essay Robert Crawford has delicately evoked Burns' younger sister, Isobel, describing her as a 'lost icon' of Scottish literature [15]. If she is known at all today, it is because her (male) contemporaries took an interest in her in connection to her famous brother, passing on to us a partial and yet intriguing portrait of a woman who could not read and write and yet, far from being uncultivated, had a wonderful mnemonic knowledge of songs and ballads and a developed 'literary' taste. A similar portrait — this time of Burns' mother — was offered by Catherine Carswell in her controversial biography of the Bard (*The Life of Robert Burns*, 1930) — a challenging work, whose hidden agenda is precisely that of 'giving voice' to the many women who had revolved around the poet — mother and sisters, friends and lovers — and whose experience had never been regarded as worth recording by male biographers:

> And as she worked she sang. Many of her songs had never been written down, others were from fleetingly printed strips picked from the barrows at Ayr or Maybole [...]; but since then they had passed so often from mouth to mouth that whole verses had been lost, and new verses added, and lines altered beyond recognition. [...]. Agnes was a good song-carrier, her voice sweet and strong, her memory excellent. [16]

As Carswell reminds us, the majority of women may have been illiterate in this historical period, but they did partake in the production of oral literature, both in the Lowlands and in the Highlands. Even though their names have not been recorded, it is only appropriate to bestow on their extensive contribution to the construction of Scottish culture that critical legitimation — as Carswell does in her *Life* — which was denied in their lifetime and, for a long time, in literary histories. Sadly, their voice cannot be retrieved.

It can be said that women in Scotland, as in other marginalised/colonised countries/regions, were silenced twice: first, in their own time, through exclusion from education and thus from the possibility of expressing themselves in other modes than the oral ones, and secondly through the marginalisation of 'orature' by the written text. The ideological frames supporting both forms of marginalisation were, in Britain as elsewhere, deeply intertwined — patriarchy and imperialism.

References

1 See Homi K. Bhabha (ed.) *Nation and Narration*, London: Routledge, 1990.

2 Some scholars have challenged the view that the pro-Union faction's motivation was mainly economic and have stressed how the Union, in fact, was to damage the economic interests of all classes in Scotland. See Paul H. Scott, *The Boasted Advantages*, Edinburgh: Saltire Society, 1999.

3 Howard Gaskill (ed.), *The Poems of Ossian and Related Works*, Edinburgh: Edinburgh University Press, 1996, pp.205-206.

4 Homi K. Bhabha, "Dissemination. Time, Narrative and the Margins of the Modern Nation", in *The Location of Culture*, London: Routledge, 1994, p.170.

5 Howard D. Weinbrot, *Britannia's Issue. The Rise of British Literature from Dryden to Ossian*, Cambridge: Cambridge University Press, 1993, p.479.

6 Ronald Black (ed.), *An Lasair. Anthology of 18th Century Scottish Gaelic Verse*, Edinburgh: Birlinn, 2001, p.xiv.

7 Kenneth Simpson, *The Protean Scot. The Crisis of Identity in 18th-century Scottish Literature*, Aberdeen: Aberdeen University Press, 1988, p.2.

8 Matthew Arnold "The Study of Poetry" (1880), in *The Complete Works of Matthew Arnold*, Ann Arbor: The University of Michigan Press, 1973, p182.

9   "Surprising effects of Original Genius, exemplified in the Poetical Production of Robert Burns, an Ayrshire Ploughman", in *The Lounger*, No. 97, 9th December 1786.

10 Macaulay: *Prose and Poetry*, G.M. Young (ed.), Cambridge, Mass.: Harvard University Press, 1952, p.729.

11 Homi K. Bhabha, "Of mimicry and man: the ambivalence of colonial discourse", in Homi K. Bhabha, *The Location of Culture*, London: Routledge, 1994, pp.85-92.

12 Jean-Jacques Rousseau, *Émile*, in *Oeuvres Complétes de Jean-Jacques Rousseau*, Paris: Bibliothéque de la Pléaiade, 1959-69, Vol.IV, p.750.

13 Kathryn Sutherland, "Adam Smith's Master Narrative: Women and the *Wealth of the Nations*", in Stephen Copley, Kathryn Sutherland (eds.), *Adam Smith's Wealth of Nations. New Interdisciplinary Essays*, Manchester: Manchester University Press, 1995, pp.97-121.

14 David Hume, "Of Chastity and Modesty", in *A Treatise of Human Nature*, L.A. Selby-Bygge (ed.), Oxford: Clarendon Press, 1978 p.573.

15 Robert Crawford, "Burns' sister", in D. Gifford, D. McMillan (eds.), *A History of Scottish Women Writers*, Edinburgh: Edinburgh University Press, 1997, pp.90-102.

16 Catherine Carswell, *The Life of Robert Burns*, Edinburgh, Canongate, 1990, p.37.

FOUR

The Land of Romance and the cracked looking-glass

We live in ideas. Through images we seek to comprehend our world. And through images we sometimes seek to subjugate and dominate others. But picture-making, imagining, can also be a process of celebration, even of liberation. New images can chase out the old.

Salman Rushdie (*Imaginary Homelands*, 1991)

Laughing again, he brought the mirror away from Stephen's peering eyes.
— The rage of Caliban at not seeing his face in a mirror, he said. If Wilde were only alive to see you.
Drawing back and pointing, Stephen said with bitterness:
— It is a symbol of Irish art. The cracked lookingglass of a servant.

James Joyce (*Ulysses*, 1922)

If the 18th century is the age of 'revolution', and thus of unsettlement and deep change, the 19th century marks the gradual consolidation of the Union and of the relations between its partners. The imperial joint venture proves to be extremely advantageous in economic terms, and the Scottish bourgeoisie has plenty of good reasons to celebrate its fledgling Britishness and to overlook the marginalisation of the vernacular aspects of its native culture — these will receive an increasingly 'domestic' and/or 'exotic' handling, which will climax, by the end of the century, in the Kailyard novels, those "literatures of domesticity and rustic humour",[1] which, somewhat unfairly, attracted the contempt of Scottish intellectuals in the following century. This does not mean that the national question is peripheral in this period — on the contrary. If there are

large rural areas of Scotland where London seems as distant and
alien as New York or New Delhi, and where a sense of identification
with the new national super-structure does not even start to take
shape until the aftermath of the First World War, even urban
Scotland, where support of the Union seems to be highest, betrays
unrest as to the new political pattern. The neat division promoted
by the Union between the 'improved' present of 'northern Britain'
and Scotland's picturesque but regressive past, may appear as a
fully accepted fact in Scottish literary texts of the period, yet a close
reading will often reveal tensions as well as strategies of resistance
to assimilation to the centre, ultimately undermining that very idea
of harmonious cohesion and integration that they purport to
promote.

The 19th century — the age of Scottish 'Ascendancy' — is an
extremely fertile period for Scottish literature, which wins
enthusiastic readers well beyond British borders: in Europe, in
north America and in the colonies, in English as well as in
translation. Sir Walter Scott and R. L. Stevenson reach a huge
reading public, all over the world, and for a long time they stand
for quintessential Scottishness. In fact, they can be said to have
fashioned and exported the two most powerful and resilient
'visions' of Scotland in the modern age — that of the 'Land of
Romance' (celebrating the romantic beauty of its wild landscape
and the picturesque charm of its ancient costumes and traditions),
and that, connected to the former, of a country of dark mysteries
and endless Gothic fascination. No surprise, then, that the 20th-
century 'Scottish Renaissance' intellectuals rejected most of the
writers of this period (Scott in particular), as guilty of the creation
and propagation of a distorted, 'colonial' image of their country.
Yet, with the benefit of hindsight, this severe judgement passed on
a whole generation of writers was quite unwise: was it really Scott's
fault if his complex representation of the Scottish past was
simplified into fixed 'clichés', conforming to the ideological
perspective of the British establishment? We may observe that the
fate of Scott's work, in this respect, is akin to that of Macpherson's

— both writers articulated effectively the problematic predicament of the writer in post-Union Scotland, both represented a distinctively Scottish voice, both reached an enormous success in terms of readership. The works of both were 'tamed' — in very different ways — into safe readings, which erased the unsettling or potentially subversive elements of their narratives.

Sir Walter Scott has been considered, with Macpherson, as one of the most influential contributors to the construction of the 'invented' Highland tradition of Scotland, remorselessly 'exposed' in a controversial essay by Hugh Trevor-Roper [2], published in 1983. Trevor-Roper, beside contending (somewhat puzzlingly) that Gaelic culture should be regarded as properly Irish and not Scottish, argues that the best known icons of the Scottish nation are based on bogus Highland symbols — the kilt and the tartan — crafted, between the end of the 18th and the beginning of the 19th century, mainly by Lowlanders. While there is some truth in Trevor Roper's reconstruction, it is certainly somewhat questionable — as it has been observed — to discriminate traditions on the grounds of their degree of 'authenticity' [3], given the symbolic and therefore arbitrary nature of their practice (should some traditions be stigmatised because they are more 'invented' than others?), and of their antiquity (is it only established European nations which can claim a 'proper' tradition?). Trevor-Roper's tone hovers between the patronising and the moralistic and is somewhat at odds with the more detached analysis offered by Eric Hobsbawm's introduction to the same collection of essays, according to which 'invented traditions' can emerge within a brief and dateable period, even in a few years, and establish themselves with great rapidity, being characterised by a set of practices of a ritual or symbolic nature "which seek to inculcate certain values and norms of behaviour by repetition, which automatically implies continuity with the past."[4] These traditions, the Highland one being a case in point, originate in the need to respond to novel situations at times of rapid or traumatic change and "take the form of reference to old situations, or . . . establish their own past by quasi-obligatory repetition."[5] Not surprisingly, then, in the age of the rise and expansion of European empires, invented traditions seem to bloom — very often created out of the encounter between colonisers and colonised. It is this very context of colonial relations into which many of these 'new' expressions of national identification develop that may encourage us to introduce a subtler perspective than that implied by Trevor-Roper. In fact, if a motivated reinvention of the past often serves the interest of the dominant power, in a different context, it may also be employed by colonised or marginalised communities as a form of resistance. As post-colonial cultural criticism has shown, there is a complex dialectic linking these parallel processes, and the case of Scotland can be regarded as eloquent in this context. This is possibly best exemplified by Sir Walter Scott's role of mastermind and architect of the national pageant held in honour of King George IV's visit to Edinburgh, in 1822: the pageant undoubtedly provided a reply to the need that the Union had produced in Scotland, that is to represent itself in a homogeneous way, compatible to the tenets of the new United Kingdom, and yet distinctively 'national'. Scott was certainly one of the most influential and successful contributors to the consolidation of the new Scottish tradition, as well as to its successive commodification, and yet the pageant should be seen as an ambivalent act — on one side it sanctioned Scotland's Britishness, on the other it set forth a set of symbols which were to serve as a line of defence against pervasive anglicisation. Pratt would describe this as an example of 'autoethnography', that is an attempt to represent oneself "in ways that engage with the coloniser's own terms" [6] — an engagement which always implies, on the part of the colonised, dialogue as well as resistance.

It is necessary to stress, however, that the establishment of the new Scottish tradition marks also the climax of a distinct act of appropriation (in this respect Trevor-Roper's remarks are truthful) on the part of the Lowlands of Highland folklore. The kilt, the woven patterns of the tartan indicating affiliation to a clan, the bagpipes — in short all the traditional markers of Scottish cultural distinctiveness have indeed been borrowed (or stolen?) from the Gaelic Highlands. The dominant Anglo-Scottish middle-class is in search of cultural icons which are markedly 'non-English' and which, at the same time, do not refer to a current practice but are safely deferrable to the 'past' (or to the 'past' represented by a distinct region). The erasure of cultural difference within Scotland and the fabrication and relocation of Scottishness outside the realm of everyday life will of course have far-reaching consequences, which will affect — as we shall see — both communities.

Scott's role as a novelist is even more problematic than that of mastermind of the pageant: a single-minded celebration of British Scotland is, in fact, even less achievable within the boundaries of a literary text — by nature polysemic and therefore inherently ambivalent. Besides, an evolution of some sort in Scott's attitude to the Union is witnessed by the sequence of his 'Jacobite' novels. If *Waverley* (1814), which has certainly received more critical attention (also due to the fact that it inaugurated the fortunate series of his historical romances), still manages to convey an idea of a harmonious solution of the tensions between the Scottish past and the British present, *Rob Roy* (1817) and, to an even greater extent, *Redgauntlet* (1824), seem more set on destabilising that harmony, by undermining the very pillars on which it rests, such as the existence of a univocal truth, the linearity of realistic narration, the clear-cut divisions between national (and even gender) identities. In *Rob Roy*, written in memoir form, the traditional 'happy ending' gives way to a mournful echo in the report made by an aged and 'paralysed' narrator/protagonist, who looks back at the events set at the time of his youth and of the 1715 Jacobite rebellion, and who seems no less incapable of telling his own story, than of taking an active role as the young protagonist of the story. Frank Osbaldistone often portrays himself as a passive victim, repeatedly rescued by his determined and decision-making friend (and future wife) Diana, in a disquieting reversal of feminine/masculine roles: the double passivity that qualifies him, the sense of unresolved anguish and failure that echoes in his words shed a dark light on the superficial resolution of conflicts (marked by the suppression of the rebellion and by the protagonist's return to his father's counting-house in England), recalled by Frank himself at the end of the novel.

Even darker, in this respect, is the ending of *Redgauntlet* — an intriguing novel, edging towards science-fiction in its purely conjectural evocation of a third Jacobite rebellion that never took place. Quashed before its beginning, the rebellion marks, on a superficial level, a definitive watershed between two worlds, as anticipated by Alan — an Edinburgh lawyer — in one of his letters to his romantic friend Darsie, who will be involuntarily involved (a little like Waverley) in the rebels' cause. Scotland has now entered, in Alan's words, the age of "civil courage", when "it is of little consequence to most men . . . whether they ever possess military courage or no" [7]: there is no longer room for romantic heroes and adventure in a 'civilised' Scotland, as battles are now safely fought in the law courts. And yet, once more, the subtle process of relativisation which has taken place in the course of three hundred pages or so renders Alan's apparently simple and univocal statement much less reassuring than it seems at first. Readers have learnt, by the end of the novel, that legal as well as historical truths are textual constructions and as such they can be modified at each successive act of 'narration', as in the highly paradigmatic law-suit Peebles vs. Stanes, where truth is continually deferred as alternative interpretations are offered by the opposing lawyers. Things are never simple in Walter Scott's novels, especially in *Redgauntlet*. Even the final triumph of (British) modernity — marked by the arrival of the government army, which easily persuades the rebels to surrender in exchange for unconditional mercy — is only a relative and temporary one. In different ways and to different degrees, the memory of the 'romance' of Scotland's heroic past haunts the reader well beyond the *finis* of the three novels and the triumph of the *pax britannica*. This is not to say, of course, that Scott was a radical or that he promoted at any level a project of political resistance, rather, his novels — officially subscribing to a 'conservative' ideal — simply by speaking, as they do, from the margins of the United Kingdom, articulate a standpoint which is inevitably at odds with the vision of the centre. Of Scott we can say what Salman Rushdie says about the migrant: having suffered displacement he suspects 'reality', and "having experienced several ways of being, he understands their illusory nature". [8] The Union does not entail the physical crossing of a frontier for Lowlanders, and yet Scott (undoubtedly a paradigmatic writer of 19th-century Scotland) crosses frontiers repeatedly in his fiction — historical, political, cultural and linguistic. Even though the form of displacement he experiences is a privileged one, compared to that of many of his contemporaries in the Highlands or in other parts of the expanding British Empire, he can be said to live on the borderline of history and language, and thus to be in a position to translate difference into "a kind of solidarity" [9] rather than into a hierarchical structure.

As Scott's relativisation of consolidated truths, his frequent destabilisation of the well-established binary oppositions (man/woman, English/Scottish, north/south, history/romance etc.) — not openly critical, and yet certainly unsettling of the imperial vision — are grounded in his experience of 'border-crossing', it is not surprising that this same attitude is shared by other Scottish writers in the 19th century, such as Susan Ferrier (1782-1854), born into an upper-middle class family in Edinburgh New Town, and author of *Marriage* (1818), one of the few examples of female *Bildungsroman* written in this period. The novel can be said to appropriate Scott's themes and techniques in a strikingly original way — the most substantial deviation being the representation of social and political tensions in the writer's present, as opposed to Scott's deferral of division and discord to the past. Furthermore, Ferrier represents the unresolved conflicts within the United Kingdom through the cross-examination of the institution which, between the 18th and the 19th century, crucially redefines women's predicament in society. As Mary Wollstonecraft had pointed out in her *Vindication of the Rights of Women* (1792), the denial of political rights, of education and of equal work seem to crystallise in the redefinition of marriage, which indeed becomes a form of "legal prostitution", insofar as it compels women to economic dependence on their husbands. The Marriage Act (1753) — around whose consequences Ferrier's novel is constructed — beside sanctioning women's state of subordination, represents the first effort to exert state control over religious marriages, and an attempt to prevent clandestine marriages which had also the tacit aim of protecting property interests and preserving inheritance through the family line. The Marriage Act did not apply in Scotland, where it was possible for young couples to get married without parental consent — Ferrier's novel aptly starts with one such act of border-crossing and social transgression, as the two young protagonists flee England and make for the nearest Scottish village in order to legitimise their relationship against their parents' will. By weaving the complex network of relations that binds her characters through time and space, Ferrier charts, like Scott, the web of tensions between the Highlands and the Lowlands, and between Scotland and England. Unlike Scott, however, she looks at them through a markedly woman's stance. *Marriage* is a woman's world — populated almost exclusively by female characters, it provides an intriguingly complex picture of 19th-century Britain's social and regional/national cultures, as well as a stunningly articulated survey of the different practices (legal or simply customary) that regulate women's public and private life in this historical period. If on one side Ferrier undoubtedly stigmatises more markedly the customs of the volatile and vacuous English upper classes than those of the dour aristocracy of the Highlands, on the other it is obvious that she points at the fact that the same (patriarchal) ideology imbues both communities — 'a man's a man for all that' at the end of the day, south or north of the Tweed. "Edication! What has her edication been, to mak her different frae other women? If a woman can nurse her bairns, mak their claes, and manage her hooss, what mair need she do?"[10] mumbles the stern Laird of Glenfern, thus neatly summarising the basics of an established male standpoint, which cuts across cultures, classes, political divisions and languages — education ('culture') is the preserve of men, while women are identified with their biological role ('nature'). They are mothers and house labourers in the Highlands, mothers and fashionable ornaments in southern England. Unlike Scott, then, Ferrier does subscribe to a project of reform — that of granting women dignity and the right to education. Her appeal — extremely similar, in substance, to that formulated by Mary Wollstonecraft — has no radical overtones, and yet, being subject to a double marginalisation — as a Scottish citizen and as a woman — Ferrier manages to articulate a definition of identity, personal as well as national, which is quite challenging, grounded as it is in the individual's fluid social and personal relations and interactions, rather than traced along 'bloodlines'. In *Marriage* the best mothers are, significantly, the adoptive rather than the natural ones (Ferrier's implicit challenge to the conventional definition of motherhood in strictly biological terms is certainly ahead of her times). Similarly, national affiliations are regulated not by birth or ancestry but by the free choice of the individual. For Ferrier's striking set of hybrid (Anglo-Scottish) characters pre-set and external models are, in fact, of little avail — as one of them explains. Her positive characters, like Emily, strive to find their own way against dominant conformism:

> I prefer an original any day to a good copy. How it shocks me to hear people recommending to their children to copy such a person's manners! A copied manner, how insupportable! The servile imitator of a set pattern, how despicable! . . .[11]

If "the machinery of the human mind" is so "intricate and unwieldy"[12], as the wise Mrs. Douglas observes, conformity can only be an act of hypocrisy, and it comes at a cost.

Yet another fascinating journey into issues of national identity is represented by a Scottish novel which, among other things, boasts the primacy of being the first British political novel. *The Member: an Autobiography* (1832), by John Galt, is what today's reviewers would classify as an 'instant book' — written in 1831, it appears in the year when the Reform Bill, which marks the end of the novel as well as of its protagonist's parliamentary adventure, is passed in

Westminster. The Bill puts an end to a series of then common and yet somewhat questionable practices among MPs, including the one merrily adopted by the main character — Archibald Jobbry — that is the 'purchase' of a small constituency in order to win a seat in Parliament. Jobbry's odd experience not only exposes the institutionalised corruption of the British Parliament (thus implicitly humbling the moral stance of a country which had the presumption to be a beacon of civilisation for its worldwide Empire), but also serves as a paradigm of the status of Scotland within the Union. Jobbry is an outsider in London, and doubly so: both as a 'Nabob', newly returned to his country after years of absence, and as a Scotsman, who does not identify with the customs and the glib language of the centre of the Empire. The novel significantly focuses on the three mandates of Jobbry's parliamentary adventure and only scant reference is made to his previous life in India or in Scotland ('regions' which remain equally marginal in the novel); when the corrupt MP is finally dismissed, he takes his leave from the reader and withdraws to Scotland — to the 'margins' where he belongs, thus reverting to his original role of "simple spectator"[13]. Archibald Jobbry is a baffling and tender character: a tightrope-walker by necessity, caught as he is in precarious balance between different codes and practices, he is pragmatically keen to learn the rules of a game he has not designed, and set to win it, beyond any logic of justice or morality. A Machiavellian gambler, he is at the same time a frail character, who, in the end, like many of Scott's characters, is overwhelmed by the tide of change. In fact, Jobbry, for most of the novel, is able to turn his deracination and his sense of not belonging anywhere into a source of strength. He shifts between roles, never identifying fully with anyone — a Nabob returned to Britain after a long time of absence, a Scotsman by birth and accent, a committed British MP, a shrewd and unscrupulous businessman. Scottishness becomes a 'mask', which he conveniently wears in order to deceive his English interlocutors and make them underestimate his skills — a good example of how stereotypes can be used against the establishment which enforces them. A telling example of this is offered by the episode where he manages to trick the competent Mr. Probe on the fixing of the price of the seat by playing the role (tongue in cheek) of the naive Scottish peasant: "I patted the side of my nose with my forefinger, and said, in the jocular words of Burns, 'But Tam kent what was what fu' brauly'". The reader can easily guess that Mr. Probe is just about to fall victim to the 'canny Scot' the exact moment he replies "'Your candour […] is exceedingly satisfactory […]'"[14]. An even more interesting example of the protagonist's exploitation of Scotland's marginality to serve his own ends, is provided by the episode where Jobbry, faced by mounting difficulties in his election campaign, decides to invite a pair of street-actors ("a mountebank and his merry-andrew") to exhibit their "skill and lofty tumblings in the market-place"[15]. These are, respectively, "a great physician from the Athens of the North, with his servant, a learned professor"[16]: two representatives of Scotland's international prestige in the world of learning and science are, then, ridiculed in the 'circus' of the election campaign, an outright act of (cultural) humiliation that Jobbry light-heartedly undertakes in order to gain personal power. His parliamentary adventure seems indeed to offer a parable of Scotland's Union history: his return to his native land, after his election defeat, at the end of the novel, is marked by a sense of bafflement and loss. Having learnt how to conform to and use to his advantage the clichés through which the centre describes his native culture, once back 'home' he discovers that they do not allow him to grasp the reality around him any longer. The dedication, which appears at the beginning of the novel, and which is obviously retrospective, provides us with a glimpse of Jobbry's new predicament — that of an exile in his own country. If at first he is able to take comfort in a country he has learnt to see as the historyless Land of Romance ("Here we might watch afar off the rolling of the popular billows, and the howlings of the wind of change and perturbation, and bide our time."[17]), in barely one day he discovers that things are not quite what they seem: "I am credibly informed that the weavers of Guttershiels, over their cups on hogmanae and yesterday, were openly discussing the division of landed properties in this district!"[18]. Social change is then about to sweep also the timeless moors of Scotland — there are no remaining fixed certainties to which Archibald Jobbry (or the reader) can anchor his life.

Scott, Ferrier and Galt can be described as conservative writers — they were undoubtedly loyal to the Union, and yet, notwithstanding their will to recentre Scotland within a new 'British' norm, and thus to conform to the standard set by the centre, they seem simply unable to provide a straightforward and faithful representation of those values which they officially uphold. By borrowing James Joyce's famous description of Irish art as "the cracked lookingglass of a servant"[19] — that is a 'servile' expression which strove, without succeeding, to reproduce the style and the contents of the colonisers' art — we may say that these writers too, in their own way, 'mimicked' the centre. And yet, as some post-colonial critics argue today, it is precisely this kind of mimicry that disrupts the colonial discourse by doubling it: the simple presence of the colonised 'Other' within the textual structure is enough evidence of the 'ambivalence' of the colonial text, an ambivalence that destabilises its claim for absolute authority or unquestionable authenticity. Scott, Ferrier and Galt, in their effort to embrace Britishness, produced literary works which deeply unsettled its cardinal principles, such as a linear progression of history, monolithic national identities, the existence of universal and univocal truths, thus revealing the limitations of the central authority — they certainly did not stage an opposition to the primacy of England within the Union, rather they subtly undermined its prestige. 19th-century Scottish literature offers numerous examples of this type of disruptive 'ambivalence' — the Scottish Renaissance intellectuals who, in the early 20th century, frowned upon their predecessors, often denouncing their servile acceptance of the vision of the centre, failed to see that the latter had located an area of considerable political and cultural uncertainty in that same structure of imperial dominance against which the former were launching their open rebellion.

The 19th-century marks, in Scotland, also the century of the Gaelic diaspora ('Fuadach nan Gàidheal'): between 1780 and 1880 the Highland Clearances and the annexed powerful economic changes force thousands of Gaels to leave their inland villages and move to the sea coast or to the industrial cities or choose emigration overseas. Their fate — one of political and cultural repression and forced emigration — is similar to that of the neighbouring Irish Gaels, with the only substantial difference that it remains painfully untold for a much longer time. In *Consider the Lilies* by Iain Crichton Smith, published in 1968, and set at the time of the Sutherland Clearances, in the 19th century, a fictional evicted peasant addresses an historical character, Patrick Sellar — the notorious factor of the Duke of Sutherland, in charge of the implementation of the forced evictions — and warns him:

> "... There are some poets, we call them bards, who have written songs about you. Did you know that? ... You see, Mr Sellar, you will become a legend. You have become a legend. Are you flattered? Is that what you wanted? You talk about the future. Yes, true enough, you too will have a future. Children will sing about you in the streets in different countries you will never visit. They may even recite poems about you in the schools. Yes, your name will be on people's lips."
> "Who reads these Gaelic poems anyway?"
> "Who, indeed? Nevertheless, they exist ..."[20]

The passage is consciously anachronistic — the 'prophecy' is a projection of a 20th-century perspective on this particular historical period and of a modern author's will to retrieve, in the literary space of his novel, the voice of the silenced Gaels. Implied, here, is also a heart-rending coming to terms with a language dilemma, faced by other Celtophone contemporary writers — the choice between writing in Gaelic, to ensure the continuation of the native tradition, or in English, in order to overcome a long-standing isolation. Iain Crichton Smith's English prose offers one of the possible solutions to this dilemma, by means of a subtle appropriation of the English language, moulded to "bear the burden of another experience"[21] as

the Nigerian writer Chinua Achebe, who also chose to write in
English rather than in his native Ibo, would say. The history of the
evicted Gaels, which has been hitherto confined to 'unreadable'
Gaelic poems, becomes, through his novel, 'visible' and available
even to distant readers. Scotland's 19th-century literary map seems
much more clear-cut and 'essentialist' in this respect: while
literature in English radically supresses the Clearances (the most
outstanding example is that offered by Sir Walter Scott's textual
repression of the Highland present), predictably, a large part of
19th-century Gaelic poetry is devoted to their toll of pain and death,
as well as to the reality of emigration. As Derick Thomson observes,
a sense of loss and of nostalgia for a lost world dominates the poetry
of this period, both from the perspective of the migrants, and of
those who remain and witness the dramatic changes which affect
their society and the environment in which they live. 'Change' is a
word ridden with grief, and it refers to something 'universal' and
irreversible, as witnessed by one of the best-known poets of this
period, Màiri Nic a' Phearsain (Mary Macpherson):

> Ach thàinig caochladh air na neòil,
> Air na cnuic is air na lòin,
> Far an robh na daoine còir',
> 'S e th' ann caoraich-mhór' is uain.
>
> *But change has come upon the clouds,*
> *on the hills and on the fields,*
> *where once kindly people lived*
> *now there are "big sheep" and lambs.*[22]

'Change' reflects — significantly — also upon 19th-century
Scottish Gaelic poetry, which is characterised by a degree of
innovation, fostered not only by the forced and more intense contact
with English culture and language — sanctioned in 1872 by the
Education Act — but also by the status of the Highlanders as a
diasporic people. The 'Gàidhealtachd' is now fragmented in an
archipelago of new communities, scattered in the Scottish
industrialised central belt, in Canada, in the USA, in the colonies;

as generations of emigrants and their descendants keep in touch with 'home', or simply preserve its memory, they contribute to the circulation of their native culture and also to its transformation by responding differently to the different historical and cultural contexts in which they now live. "Change without sound, yet change nonetheless, and change that was important"[23] is how Alistair MacLeod, in *No Great Mischief* (1999), describes this gradual process of alteration in one such community, a Cape Breton 'clan', founded in 1799 by a Calum MacDonald, migrated from the Highlands with his twelve children and a faithful dog. MacLeod — a Canadian writer of international renown, himself of Highland origin and brought up in Nova Scotia — articulates a vision of the Gaelic diaspora that is very unlike anything that has been written in Scotland. Migration does not entail only 'loss', but also the opening up of novel lines of exchange and connection, as well as new, shared memories. "Do you remember?" is the question that members of *clann Chalum Ruaidh* keep asking each other in MacLeod's novel. The reply may be 'yes', or 'no', or, in the main character and narrator's words: "I'm not sure how many of the memories are real and how many I've sort of made up from other people's stories"[24]. Voices intersect and overlap in the novel, and for the reader it is impossible to remember or track the origin of the stories narrated, as these take on a life of their own and the act of remembering itself gives shape and meaning to the surrounding reality:

> Sometimes those gathered would merely watch the fire and its shadows, but at other times it seemed to move them to tell stories of real or imagined happenings from the near or distant past. And if the older singers or storytellers of the *clann Chalum Ruaidh*, the *seanaichies*, as they were called, happened to be present they would 'remember' events from a Scotland which they had never seen, or see our future in the shadows of the flickering flames. [25]

Memory, individual and collective, on which the oral transmission of native culture was largely based in the Highlands, is thus thematised in Gaelic literature, starting from the 19th century onwards, as a direct response to the erasure of the Highland civilisation by the Anglo-Scottish establishment.

It is necessary, at this stage, to widen the scope of the discussion of the 'Celtic question' from a strictly Scottish context to a British one, and it is equally important to bear in mind that the treatment reserved to the Highlands is, in this very historical period, emblematic of what takes place in many British colonies: cultural diversity is either stigmatised as a sign of backwardness, as in Matthew Arnold's notorious construction of the Celt as the 'Other', or exoticised, as in Scott's historical novels, which 'invent' a new Highland reality, standing for and by the Lowland present. The two perspectives are obviously intertwined, even though the former writer's outlook is decidedly less sympathetic than the latter's. Matthew Arnold, Professor of Poetry at the University of Oxford, was writing about the Celts from a safe distance, as it were, his only concern being that of presenting their literature as a valuable, if flawed, contribution to an otherwise superior culture. Scott's stance, even though not dissimilar from Arnold's, is, as we have seen, more problematic, in so far as he used the Highland past to forge Scotland's traditions in the present. Scott certainly experienced a degree of identification with his Highlanders (of the 'the-way-we-were' type), whereas Arnold's condescending portrait of the Celt as indolent, irresponsible, garrulous, mystical and passionate, with a predilection for alcohol, music and lost causes, as opposed to the Saxon's industrious, responsible, taciturn, pragmatic and phlegmatic nature and his predilection for sobriety, statistics and success (all the definitions are taken from his various writings on the subject), represent an unwavering and conclusive assessment. His binary distinction of the Saxon and Celtic 'races' will influence generations of English and Scottish critics and readers, and will provide a resilient ideological framework for overtly racist proclamations (especially in the late 19th-century anti-Irish wave) or an inspiration for expressions of cloudy Celticism, which opposed to the grim reality of industrialised society a "shadowy Land of Heart's Desire"[26]. The Highlander

William Sharp/'Fiona MacLeod', at the turn of the century, provides a telling example of this attitude — in an essay entitled "Celtic" he reinstates quite firmly the binary distinction Saxon/Celt:

> Even in those characteristics which distinguish Celtic literature — intimate natural vision; a swift emotion that is sometimes a spiritual ecstasy, but sometimes is also a mere intoxication of the senses; a peculiar sensitiveness to the beauty of what is remote and solitary; a rapt pleasure in what is ancient and in the contemplation of what holds an indwelling melancholy; a visionary passion for beauty... — even in these characteristics it does not stand alone, and perhaps not pre-eminent. [27]

Beside summarising all the features commonly attributed to the Celts, he ends up with a telling act of subordination (somewhat anticipated by his choice of a feminine literary pseudonym): "As for literature, there is, for all of us, only, English literature. All else is provincial or dialectic."[28] Dr. Johnson and Arnold's lesson has indeed gone home.

There is of course a deep interrelation between the romanticisation of the Highlands (both as 'space' and as 'history'), and the exploitation of this region as a favourite tourist destination. The tourism industry, that is the commodification of cultural diversity (codified as exotic), which characterises on a large scale the modern and post-modern era, cannot, in fact, be separated from the colonial legacy. Caren Kaplan, for example, has pointed out that it is a long-term outcome of colonialism that the destabilising or resisting elements of the 'Other' are fixed into 'vanishing', 'endangered' and 'local' features,[29] thus becoming an attractive location for travellers/tourists in search of the 'authenticity' or 'purity' of a 'lost' or remote culture — a purity which is not attainable in the modern world any longer. The aura of nostalgic melancholia that permeates the Anglo-Scottish taste for this remote and 'impervious' region partakes then of that 'imperialist nostalgia' which extended to distant and different colonised territories (like Kipling's sensual India, or Haggard's mysterious Africa), and which has been so effectively described in the words of Renato Rosaldo:

> A person kills somebody, and then mourns the victim . . . , somebody deliberately alters a form of life, and then regrets that things have not remained as they were prior to the intervention . . . , people destroy their environment, and then they worship nature. In any of its versions, imperialist nostalgia uses a pose of 'innocent yearning' both to capture people's imaginations and to conceal its complicity with often brutal domination. [30]

The charm that the Highlands exerts on British travellers and tourists in the 19th and 20th century is largely of this type. The ecstatic description of wild landscapes, filtered through the lens of Macpherson and Scott's literary imagination, the admiration of Scotland's monuments of 'barbarous' ages, the anecdotal reconstructions of its ancient history, and the sympathetic and yet 'anthropological' representation of its natives featured in many travel journals, betray the imperial perspective from which they are articulated. A case in point is that offered by J.E. Bowman's *The Highlands and Islands. A Nineteenth-Century Tour* (1827), a travel journal where the 'simple virtue' of the primitive Highlanders is often juxtaposed with the more civilised and therefore corrupt southern neighbours — an effective illustration of Ronsaldo's 'imperialist nostalgia':

> A stout and rather short Highlander with swarthy complexion and black hair, and having more of the Celtic character than I had yet seen, was fetching water to boil his oatmeal. . . I expressed some surprize, and his civil and open demeanour emboldened me to ask if they had no animal food, bread, or potatoes? Nor was it lessened when he said that their sole food was 'porridge', or oatmeal and water, seasoned with a little salt. Upon such simple food do these hardy people labour hard and brave the rigours of the Scotch winter! A powerful lesson to the pampered inhabitants of England, more than one half of whose diseases are the offspring of luxury and indolence. [31]

Travellers in the 19th century, just like tourists in our age, cross boundaries, figuratively or physically, in search of emotions and adventure — their movements, in fact, far from being transgressive, contribute to the construction and reinforcement of those same boundaries, and also of the hegemonic relations between the cultures which they demarcate. Not unlike other journals of the same period, Bowman's describes the return home (to England) in terms of a celebration of domesticity:

> . . . on the conclusion of this Tour, I return with a more expanded goodwill to all mankind, an increased sense of esteem to my immediate friends, a redoubled affection for the one who accompanied me, a confirmed love toward all my family endearments, and a higher sense of duty for his protection to the Great Father of all, the Author and Giver of all good things. [32]

The experience of travel has perhaps broadened the author's own spiritual horizon — as he claims — but it has, above all, reinforced the *status quo*.

The literary text becomes, then, the privileged site for the new constructions of Celtic identity, of the Highland past and of the Highland landscape. It is not too difficult to surmise a 'complicity' between English and (Anglo-) Scottish authors in this enterprise — a prelude to the active cooperation between the same parties in the building of the British Empire.

References

1 George Blake, *Barrie and the Kailyard School*, London: Arthur Barker, 1951, p.16.

2 Hugh Trevor-Roper, "The Invention of Tradition: The Highland Tradition of Scotland", in Eric Hobsbawm, Terence Ranger (eds.), *The Invention of Tradition*, Cambridge: Cambridge University Press, 1992, pp.15-41.

3 See Cairns Craig, "Absences, in Cairns Craig, *Out of History, Narrative Paradigms in Scottish and British Culture*, Edinburgh: Polygon, 1996, pp. 108-112.

4 Eric Hobsbawm, "Introduction: Inventing Traditions", in Eric Hobsbawm, Terence Ranger (eds.), *The Invention of Tradition*, Cambridge: Cambridge University Press, 1992, p.1.

5 Ibid., p.2.

6 Mary Louise Pratt, *Imperial Eyes. Travel Writing and Transculturation*, London: Routledge, 1992, p.7.

7 Sir Walter Scott, *Redgauntlet*, Oxford: Oxford University Press, 1985, p.47.

8 Salman Rushdie, "The Location of Brazil", in Salman Rushdie, *Imaginary Homelands*, London: Granta, 1991, p.125.

9 Homi K. Bhabha, "Dissemination. Time, Narrative and the Margins of the Modern Nation", in Homi K. Bhabha (ed.) *The Location of Culture*, London: Routledge, 1994, p.170.

10 Susan Ferrier, *Marriage*, Oxford: Oxford University Press, 1997, pp.68-69.

11 Ibid., p.444.

12 Ibid., p.158.

13 John Galt, *The Member: An Autobiography*, Edinburgh: Scottish Academic Press, The Association for Scottish Literary Studies, 1985 , p.121.

14 Ibid., p.10.

15 Ibid., p.45.

16 Ibid., p.45.

17 Ibid., p.2.

18 Ibid., p.2.

19 James Joyce, *Ulysses*, Harmondsworth: Penguin, 1969, pp.12-13.

20 Iain Crichton Smith, *Consider the Lilies*, Edinburgh: Canongate, 1987, p.106.

21 Chinua Achebe, *Morning yet on Creation Day*, New York: Doubleday, 1975, p.62.

22 "Soraidh leis an Nollaig ùir"/"Farewell to the New Christmas", (translated. by Derick Thomson), in Derick Thomson, *An Introduction to Gaelic Poetry*, Edinburgh: Edinburgh University Press, 1990, p.246.

23 Alistair MacLeod, *No Great Mischief*, London: Vintage, 2001, p.67.

24 Ibid., p.12.

25 Ibid., p.60.

26 'Fiona MacLeod', "Celtic", in *The Winged Destiny. Studies in the Spiritual History of the Gael*, New York: Duffield, 1910, p.198.

27 Ibid., pp.191-192.

28 Ibid., pp.195-196.

29 Caren Kaplan, *Question of Travel. Postmodern Discourses of Displacement*, Durham and London: Duke University Press, 1996, pp.58-59.

30 Renato Rosaldo, *Culture and Truth. The Remaking of Social Analysis*, Boston: Beacon Press, 1989, pp.69-70.

31 J.E. Bowman's *The Highlands and Islands. A Nineteenth-Century Tour*, Gloucester: Alan Sutton (New York: Hippocrene Books) 1986, pp.51-52.

32 Ibid., p.204.

FIVE

Rule Caledonia:
the ambiguous relation with Empire

There is no document of civilisation which is not at the same time a document of barbarism.

Walter Benjamin ("Theses on the Philosophy of History", 1955)

In Henry Mackenzie's *Man of Feeling* (1771), Harley, the candid character who mesmerised contemporary readers with his simple heart and true sentiments, makes — towards the end of the novel — a long and articulated assessment of the colonial occupation of India:

> You tell me of immense territories subject to the English: I cannot think of their possessions without being led to inquire by what right they possess them; [...] what title have the subjects of another kingdom to establish an empire in India? to give laws to a country where the inhabitants received them on the terms of friendly commerce? You say they are happier under our regulations than under the tyranny of their petty princes. I must doubt it, from the conduct of those by whom these regulations have been made. [...] You describe the victories they have gained; they are sullied by the cause in which they fought: you enumerate the spoils of those victories; they are covered with the blood of the vanquished. [1]

Harley's remarks, inspired as they are by an innate goodness, unspoiled by the trammels of the conventional beliefs and customs that vitiate life in the modern age, reveal a strong empathy with the colonised subjects and an aversion for the contradictory rhetoric of the Empire — glorifying its 'civilising' mission and at the same time celebrating its sanguinary military feats — as well as a contempt for its unstated, true objective, that is, the economic exploitation of the conquered territories. While the force of Harley's indictment of imperialism is attenuated by the conventional context in which it is formulated — that of a highly stylised 18th-century sentimental novel, focussed on the individual's capacity to identify with and respond to the sorrows of others, rather than with a genuine desire to redress the wrongs which are the source of such sorrows — still, the length and the emphasis of the narrator's anti-colonial statement undoubtedly betray a special concern for these matters on the part of the author.

The passage is remarkable also insofar as it provides an early example of the (mainly Scottish) tendency to identify the evil-doings of the British Empire with England only, rather than with all its active partners — a perspective which became more rooted in the early 20th century, when many Scottish intellectuals, who staged a reaction against a pervasive Anglocentrism, also adopted a firmly anti-imperial stance. This identification was far from being correct, especially as far as the above region was concerned. The presence of Scots in India in the 18th century, in fact, was conspicuous, and it was certainly well established by the time Mackenzie's novel was published—it included army men, administrators, and also merchants. The British army was, incidentally, led by a Scotsman —Major General David Baird — when, in 1799, it defeated the most celebrated leader of the Indian resistance, Tipu Sultan, or 'the Tiger of Mysore', thus securing the political control of the country. General Baird was much glorified in his native country, as a 'local hero' and as incontrovertible evidence of the essential contribution that Scotland was making to the building and the expansion of the Empire. A whole popular epic was constructed around his military feats and his audacity — the valour of the 'Thistle' was thus proudly measured against the greatness of the defeated 'Tiger', a glory which still clings to the commemorations of the event, as an interesting exhibition, recently held at the National Gallery of Scotland on the occasion of the bicentenary of the British victory,[2] has shown. In the 19th century the Scottish presence in India increased, as the colony became a 'natural' outlet for many in search of fortune or a better life: "the Corn Chest for Scotland" — as Sir Walter Scott described it — "where we poor gentry must send our younger sons" [3]. Those who grew rich in the East India Company, often came back home to find themselves strangers at home, admired or scorned by their fellow countrymen. In Sir Walter Scott's *Saint Ronan's Well* there is a telling definition of a Nabob as one who "comes frae foreign parties, with mair siller than his pouches can haud, and spills it a' through the country — they are as yellow as orangers, and maun hae a' thing their ain gate"[4]. But Indian 'returnees' also included civil servants, soldiers of fortune, people who had not necessarily improved their social or financial position, and who nonetheless became familiar and distinctive figures in the Scottish society of the 19th century. Not surprisingly, literary texts from this period are scattered with portraits, often satirical, of this new class of 'misfits' — as in Henry Mackenzie's *The Lounger*, John Galt's *The Member*, Sir Walter Scott's *Guy Mannering*, and *The Surgeon's Daughter*, to mention but a few. The Empire and the involvement that Scots had in it was more than a thematic echo in 19th-century Scottish literature, it was the 'reality' against which the Scottish nation was forging and redefining itself within the United Kingdom. The myth of the 'Scottish Empire' becomes a staple component of Scottish identity and it will be a hard task indeed for intellectuals in the 20th century to discard its vestiges (and its associated collusion with England) and the deeply ingrained frame of references connected to it.

The imperial adventure of Scotland had, in fact, started well before the Union of Parliaments, when the Scots attempted to plant a settlement on the isthmus of Panama — the so-called Darien scheme, the first embryo of a Scottish commercial dominion overseas. The eventual failure of the project, in 1699, ushered in the Union, and the joint venture of the British Empire. The roots of Scottish imperialism, however, reach back even farther than the 17th century — an attentive survey of the history of Scottish culture and philosophy will reveal a more deeply ingrained attitude to colonial expansion than many scholars and observers have been ready to admit in recent times. For example in Scotland, as in other European countries, starting from the 15th century, there is a growing effort to describe the 'races of men' and to classify them according to a hierarchical principle — which leads, ultimately, to the justification of the subjugation of the peoples deemed as inferior. Racism is a powerful ideology, which cuts across national borders in the 19th century and which has in Scotland some of its most persuasive and influential forefathers, starting from John Mair, who, in the 16th century, provided an apology of the Spanish conquest of the New World and articulated an openly anti-Judaic stance [5], and continuing with David Hume, who, in a notorious footnote to his essay "Of National Characters" (1785), theorised the biological superiority of the whites:

> I am apt to suspect the Negroes to be naturally inferior to Whites. There scarcely ever was a civilised nation of that complexion, nor even any individual eminent either in action or speculation. No ingenious manufactures amongst them, no arts, no sciences. . . . Such a uniform and constant difference could not happen, in so many countries and ages, if nature had not made an original distinction between these breeds of men. . . . In Jamaica, indeed, they talk of one Negro as a man of parts and learning; but it is likely he is admired for slender accomplishments, like a parrot who speaks a few words plainly. [6]

Hume's ideas, especially those pertaining to the inferiority of Africans, were shared on the continent by Voltaire, and were later adopted also by Kant and Hegel. In Scotland they found their ideal continuation in the 19th century in the anthropological studies of George Combe who, in *A System of Phrenology* (1825), provided 'scientific evidence' for Hume's conjectures on the African races. The Scottish anatomist, Robert Knox, in *The Race of Men* (1850), aimed to demonstrate that race is the sole determinant of history and that each race expresses a distinct form of civilisation — he also promoted a fiercely anti-Semitic ideology. A similar stance was maintained by Thomas Carlyle, in his notorious pamphlet on "The Nigger Question"(1849), an eloquent example of how an anti-slavery stance did not always and necessarily imply an anti-colonial view:

> [. . .] my obscure Black friends, your work, and the getting of you set to it, is a simple affair; and by diligence, the West-Indian legislatures, and Royal governors, setting their faces fairly to the problem, will get it done. You are not 'slaves' now; nor do I wish, if it can be avoided, to see you slaves again: but decidedly you have to be servants to those that are born wiser than you, that are born lords of you; servants to the Whites, if they are (as what mortal can doubt they are?) born wiser than you. [7]

These are of course just some of the most influential voices of a much wider debate. Even though they cannot be said to speak for the whole of Scotland, which also fostered a democratic tradition, expressed, for example, in George Buchanan's inflexible indictment of colonialism, in Francis Hutcheson's firm opposition to slavery and in the numerous anti-slavery movements which flourished in the 19th century, they undoubtedly represent a substantial thread running through it, which should in no way be underestimated or discounted. Hume, Combe, Knox, Carlyle, in their respective ages, were extremely influential well beyond the borders of their native country and of Britain — it is then necessary to emphasise that the imperial enterprise, far from being a mere consequence of the Union, and of England's influence on Scotland, was largely the outcome of an endogenous movement. In this sense Scotland does not differ substantially from England or from the other European countries which, in the same period, shared similar political and ideological frameworks.

Yet, in the 19th century, the imperial discourse in Scotland is in many ways distinctive, if compared to that developing in England at about the same time. The first noteworthy feature is represented by the fact that the definition of Scottishness in this period — as partly anticipated — is deeply connected with the role played by Scotland in the building of the British Empire. It is in fact within the Empire — in its bureaucratic and military structures, as well as in the economic exploitation of its colonies — that the Scots find the most formidable outlet for the expression of their national identity. Not only were they allowed to 'export' their traditional institutions — both the Scottish legal and education systems, for example, still inform many of the ex-colonies today — but they were also offered the opportunity to celebrate a 'unified' national identity, based on those values and traits which proved most useful to the expansion and welfare of the Empire — the Scots' military prowess, their enterprising nature and bravery in face of adversity are still today celebrated virtues of the Scottish nation. The 'Other' (as in the case of the myth surrounding the clash between the 'Thistle' and the 'Tiger') becomes then subservient to the construction of Scotland's identity, following a process well known to post-colonial countries, that is of a polarisation of the 'removed' or undesirable features of its culture. In Sir Walter Scott's *The Surgeon's Daughter*, for example, India is seen as destined to inherit Scotland's exotic status of 'Land of Romance':

> "But, to tell you the truth, I think you might do with your Muse of Fiction, as you call her, as many an honest man does with his own sons in flesh and blood."
> "And how is that, my dear sir?"
> "Send her to India, to be sure. That is the true place for a Scot to thrive in; and if you carry your story fifty years back, as there is nothing to hinder you, you will find as much shooting and stabbing there as ever was in the wild Highlands . . ." [8]

To Croftanger's objection "I have never been there, and know nothing at all about them", Fairscribe replies reassuringly: "Nonsense, my good friend. You will tell us about them all the better that you know nothing of what you are saying. . . " [9]. This might be interpreted as a tongue-in-cheek confession on the part of Scott, who, in the words of R.L. Stevenson, "never knew the Highlands; he was always a Borderer. He has missed that whole, long, strange, pathetic story of our savages . . ." [10]

Imperialism is a popular movement in 19th-century Scotland, and it is not surprising to find that its most straightforward expression is indeed contained in popular forms of literature. The Kailyard novels may provide a case in point, even though they are strictly set in a secluded and rural Scotland, apparently isolated from the rest of the world. Regarded today as 'low literature', understandably despised by the Scottish Renaissance generation on the grounds of their being "literatures of domesticity and rustic humour"[11], they unquestionably represent an outstanding literary phenomenon in the 19th century, notably for the enthusiastic response of the reading public in Scotland, England, the USA and Canada. Even R.L. Stevenson admired them greatly — he had not hesitated to include Barrie among his own "Muses Three", beside Henry James and Kipling.[12] The key to the success of the novels by 'Ian Maclaren', S.R. Crockett and James Barrie lies undoubtedly in the fact that they construct a vision of Scotland which is unified and safe and which promotes the essential values of the Empire without ever representing the complex (and often disquieting) social and political circumstances produced by them. A good insight into this genre, whose aesthetical merits should not be underestimated[13], may be offered by the reassuring gaze over the quintessential Scottish village provided by the elderly narrator of *A Window in Thrums* (1889):

> Carts pass up and down the brae every few minutes, and there comes an occasional gig. Seldom is the brae empty, for many live beyond the top of it now, and men and women go to their work, children to school or play. Not one of the children I see from the window to-day is known to me, and most of the men and women I only recognise by their likeness to their parent. . . . but this I know, that the grandparents of most of these boys and girls were once young with me. If I see the sons and daughters of my friends grown old, I also see the grandchildren spinning the peerie and hunkering at I-dree-I-dree — I-droppit-it — as we did long ago. The world remains as young as ever. The lovers that met on the commonty in the gloaming are gone, but there are other lovers to take their place, and still the commonty is here. . . . The world does not

age. The hearse passes over the brae and up the straight burying-ground road, but still there is a cry for the christening robe. [14]

In a typical transfer process, the ideological values which imbue the Victorian middle class are deflected to represent an idealised rural congregation, safely located outside space and time, sheltered from the fast changes of modern society. Ideals of order and stability, expressed in set hegemonic social and gender relations are central to this popular genre, focussed as it is on the iconic representation of the village as a close-knit community, living harmoniously under the good-hearted rule of the Parish elders. [15] However, as has been rightly pointed out, Kailyard novels are also 'narratives of nation', and the stereotyped set of characters which populate them embody a defined set of features which were perceived, or became so, as distinctive of Scottishness within and without their country of origin. Endowed with moral and physical fortitude, self-reliant, enterprising, frugal, the Highlander becomes the epitome of the Scottish coloniser — a little like the way in which the enterprising Robinson Crusoe had embodied (in a much more explicit manner) English middle class imperial aspirations in the 18th century.

The resilience and dissemination of the imperial vision in 19th-century constructions of Scottishness is testified also by another immensely popular form of entertainment — the Scottish music hall. The history of this genre is inextricably linked with Glasgow — a fast-growing industrial centre in this period — and with the tastes and demands of a mainly working-class audience, and yet many of the icons produced and diffused by the music hall received a widespread (national and international) approval as symbols of Scottish nationality.[16] Harry Lauder, and the other kilted comics who followed in his footsteps, like Jock Mills and Donald McKay, were just as popular in Scotland as they were in the rest of the English-speaking world and, with the Kailyarders, they provided a resilient image of modern Scotland. It often happens that the icons of a phase of a country's cultural history survive the contingencies in which they are produced: Lauder's 'shortbread tin tartanry' is a case in point, as it has lived on well beyond the hey-day of the Empire, along with the evergreen myth of 'Scottish humour'. [17] Furthermore, as Paul Maloney has remarked, "two key elements of the Scotch comic persona — the use of tartan and the perception of the Highlander as the archetype of Scottish identity — were to feature extensively in Scottish songs promoting the cause of empire in the 1890s."[18] In fact, beyond the propaganda with which this genre soon became infused (in Scotland as well as in England), addressed, as it was, to a mass audience whose faith in the goodness of the imperial enterprise and loyalty to the Queen and the country had to be continually reinforced, the figure of the Scotch comic did undoubtedly polarise feelings of national identity in an historical period when other expressions were discouraged or stigmatised[19]. Understandably, all these popular icons were rejected by successive generations as an anti-intellectual and anti-cultural representation of Scottishness, and a clear sign of Scotland's 'Inferiorism', that is — in Franz Fanon's terminology — of an interiorised mistrust of native culture, inculcated by a repressive, imperial centre [20]. In fact, with hindsight, it would be a wrong and dangerous simplification to erase or undervalue them in a literary history of Scotland, as they witness the ambiguous stance of a country fully and proudly involved in the building of the Empire, and at the same time, culturally subordinated to England. It is this in-built ambiguity — predictably an embarassing contradiction for many a left-wing intellectual in the 20th century, who dismissed the imperial enterprise as an 'English' concern — that, ultimately, constitutes Scotland's distinctive predicament in the modern age.

A second distinctive strain in the Scottish imperial discourse — strictly connected to the first — is the opening up of moments of (at least partial) identification with the colonised subjects, matched against Scotland's history of marginality within Britain. It is a complex attitude, that does not necessarily entail an open indictment of imperialism, even less so a rejection of the Union. A very early expression of this attitude is offered by an abolitionist play with a very marked Scottish twist, *The Negro Slaves* (1799) — "a

dramatic piece, of one act, with songs" by Archibald MacLaren —
where the most outspoken and firmest advocate for the cause of
abolition is a Scotsman, McSympathy, who speaks Scots, while the
airs and ballads, included those sung by the black slave Quako, are
all Scottish[21]. The fact that Quako, whose fight for freedom
McSympathy energetically supports, speaks better English than
his Scottish friend, is surely meant to provide comic relief, but it
also hints, implicitly, at the marginal predicament of Scottish
culture/language within the United Kingdom. MacSympathy's
Scottishness, then, seems to make him more apt to 'sympathise'
with a subjugated native:

> *MacSympathy*   Quako, you speak the English language amaist as
> weel as I do my sel, wha taught you the pronunciation sae weel?
>
> *Quako*   A good, dear friend . . . An Englishman taught me to
> read and write. But his eyes are shut, and the whites have laid him in
> the cold ground. Every morning before I go to work, and every evening
> when I've finished my labour, I visit his grave, to thank his dear cold
> dead body for his kindness; but his ears are stopt, he cannot hear me,
> he cannot hear his poor unhappy Quako, when he tells him that master
> sells his hapless Sela. (weeps) [22]

Quako is educated and intelligent, beside being endowed with
a good heart and sensibility — a real 'gentleman', by the century's
tenets. In this respect he towers, morally as well as intellectually,
above any other white character in the play. Even though the author
indulges in a sentimental rhetoric, conforming to the aesthetic
canons of the period, and the piece cannot be said to articulate a
proper anti-colonial stance, it is nonetheless remarkable in so far
as it subverts the patronising myth of the 'good savage', often
resorted to by abolitionists — and it does so from an unequivocally
Scottish stance.

The establishment of paths of sympathy between Scotland and
other colonised countries was, at least partly, encouraged by the
work of a popular and internationally renowned writer like Sir
Walter Scott. His frequent comparison of the Highlanders' way of

life with that of other 'exotic' peoples, colonised by the British, certainly must have struck the imagination of readers within and without his native country. As we have seen, his historical novels stage an appropriation of Highland folklore, whose stylised version becomes a celebrated icon of Scottish culture – the affinity established between Scotland's near past and other 'primitive' cultures then, is likely to instil in the Scottish reader a sense, if not of identification, at least of contiguity with them. There is no doubt that such a sense of affinity did strike many (non-Scottish) readers in the colonies, who found Scott's Highlanders suggestive of their own predicament, while, more in general, the articulation of a cultural and linguistic distinctiveness in Scottish literature encouraged 'lines of resistance', political and cultural, across the British Empire. Tiyo Soga (1829-1871), for example, a native of the Cape Colony, ordained as a Minister of the United Presbyterian Church and the first black missionary among Africans, uses words which are revealing in this sense:

> I have not seen, but I have heard and read, of the Scottish Highlanders' love and attachment to their hereditary native chiefs. I trust the present Scottish races do not 'laugh this sentiment to scorn' because they are now under one benign rule with the English people. Whatever it was once, it kept the Highland world together, and kept the patriotism alike alive, and for that reason alone was to be admired. The Caffres are bound to their chiefs by the same devoted attachment. The addresses of the native Christians to Kreli, the hereditary head of themselves, and to his heathen people, evinced the wonderful tenderness of Christian feeling and love of race. They urged them to burst through the barriers of Caffre customs and the wiles of superstitious observances, and to open their country to a yet wider diffusion and extension of the gospel. They told them that a nation that will not educate its youth must go backwards — that it cannot advance. [23]

Educated in Scotland —he was one of the first black students at Glasgow University — and married to a Scottish woman who moved with him to live in South Africa, Tiyo Soga manifested a lifelong affection for this country, its culture and its people — he had, in fact, come to regard it as a "second home"[23]. That in his attempt to reconcile the Christian and western values with the traditional African ones, which he upheld firmly as intrinsically noble (he is regarded today as one of the fathers of the Black consciousness movement), he chooses to refer to Highland history as a model for his country, can be easily ascribed to his Scottish education. As in other instances, the perceived similarity in historical background opens up paths of sympathy and mutual understanding.

In Scotland, R.L. Stevenson provides perhaps the most radical realisation of this potential identification between Scots and the colonised peoples, by his overt siding with the natives, to the extent of becoming one of them — 'Tusitala', the story-teller, as he was nicknamed by his Polynesian friends. *The Vailima Letters* (1895) often testify to this special relation and describe the writer's active bond of friendship with the natives:

> As soon as he was finally liberated, Poe called a meeting of his fellow-prisoners. [...] He said that they had been in prison, that I had always taken an interest in them, that they had now been set at liberty without condition [...], and that this had set them considering what they might do to testify their gratitude. They had therefore agreed to work upon my road as a free gift. [...] Think of it! It is road-making — the most fruitful cause (after taxes) of all rebellions in Samoa, a thing to which they could not be wiled with money nor driven by punishment. It does give me a sense of having done something in Samoa after all. [25]

In the South Seas (1889) contains a chapter which throws a more than metaphorical bridge between Scottish (Lowland and Highland) culture and the Marquesan one — a similar history, common features of social grace and sensibility, and even (much less predictably) of language are highlighted by the author:

> Hospitality, tact, natural fine manners, and a touchy punctilio, are common to both races: common to both tongues the trick of dropping medial consonants. . . . The elision of medial consonants . . . is no less

common both in Gaelic and the Lowland Scots. Stranger still, that prevalent Polynesian sound, the so-called catch, written with an apostrophe, and often or always the gravestone of a perished consonant, is to be heard in Scotland to this day. . . . These points of similarity between a South Sea people and some of my own folk at home ran much in my head in the islands; and not only inclined me to view my fresh acquaintances with favour, but continually modified my judgement.[26]

Here, as elsewhere, Stevenson seems to go beyond Scott's sense of affinity based on "the-way-we-were" model (which nonetheless informs his writing and which undoubtedly represents a point of departure for his own undertaking) to establish a more defined and contemporary sense of 'sharing' — a dialogic rapport between the two cultures. The insistence on elements of sameness in the Polynesian and the Scottish languages, in particular, hints at an immediate, 'metonymic' contiguity between the two cultures, and indeed configures an almost 'tangible' possibility of communication. Stevenson's undertaking of the writing of a *History of Samoa* (eventually published as *A Footnote to History. Eight Years of Trouble in Samoa*, 1892), as well as his more general views on history and historiography are also very interesting in this respect: on one side he appears to be firmly rooted in the Scottish tradition ("Now Scotch is the only History I know; it is the only history represented in my library"[27] he explains to his friend Colvin, in describing his project about 'A History for Children'), on the other he clearly distances himself from it. Unlike Scott, for example, who "never knew the Highlands", he lives his daily life with Samoans and he learns their customs and their language. Stevenson remains pessimistic, however, about the response his work will have among 'western' readers — he seems very aware of their disregard for a people who, from their perspective, are seen as historyless, or, at the most, a mere 'footnote' to European history:

Will any one read it? I fancy not; people don't read history for reading, but for education and display — and who desires education in the history of Samoa, with no population, no past, no future, or the exploits of Mataafa, Malietoa, and Consul Knappe? . . . Well, it can't be helped, and it must be done for better or for worse . . . There are two to whom I have not been kind — German Consul Becker and English Captain Hand, R.N. [28]

Many Scottish writers and intellectuals followed in Stevenson's ideological footsteps. Among these, at least a short reference should be made to a woman who is remembered neither as a creative writer nor as an 'intellectual' — her name belongs today mainly to the rich production of Scottish missionary literature of the 19th century. Nicknamed somewhat inappropriately the 'White Queen' by those who were keener to canonise a 'saint' than to recognise the highly innovative elements of her experience in West Africa, Mary Slessor's distinctive and independent approach to cultural diversity has only recently been re-evaluated. To begin with, she regarded herself as a 'Mother', and not a 'Queen'. If, on the one hand, this perpetuated the patronising stereotype of the colonised subject seen as a 'child', on the other it stressed the strong relational aspect of her mission. She did not show much pride in her whiteness, nor a special admiration for the civilisation that the whites were keen to impose on their African subjects:

You must not expect to get *proper* letters for I am so busy, and if I was "slim at home" I am not so here. I laughed out right at that. I have grown stouter here, perhaps, but so *white*. We are all *whites* and no mistake. I *cannot blush now*, if I were ever so willing. [29]

She came to identify Calabar (the remote Nigerian district where she spent most of her life) as 'home' and, rather than perceiving herself as a foreigner, she considered herself as a full member of the communities in which she lived. Most of her life was spent in helping African women gain autonomy from their strongly patriarchal native society. This was carried out in full independence from the Mission, which did not always approve of her methods, especially of her choice of a practical, rather than a predominantly religious education for her 'daughters', and of her respect for African customs and laws, which she did not find intrinsically barbarous, except in their lack of Christian morality. Her numerous letters, written to friends, collaborators, authorities, practically unknown, certainly are more revealing of her outlook than most of the hagiographic records of her missionary achievements. As Cheryl McEwan has observed, for Mary Slessor the 'heart of darkness' was not represented by Africa, but by her native Europe, overshadowed by the approaching world war.[30] Her style reveals at times a striking literary sensitivity, which can only make us regret that most of her letters and papers, when not destroyed, have remained unpublished:

> If you saw the lovely pearl sky in the dawn! The earth all refreshed and cooled, and all the hope and mystery of a new day opening out, you would enjoy it as I am doing. With you and with our poor army and navy it will be darkness and cold, and probably fog, besides all the nerve-racking strain of war and long watching. With us it is all brightness and beauty with long summer months opening out before us. [31]

Naomi Mitchison's collaboration with the Bakgatla, in Botswana, as a 'tribal mother' and adviser — started in the 1960s and extended through all her life — is in many ways a continuation of Slessor's dialogic approach. She articulates a very similar wish to communicate and interact with the 'Other' or, as she phrased it, to construct those "bridges which will allow communication where none existed before or where it had gone wrong".[32] Like Slessor, Mitchison also believed that "Africa can give a lead"[33], as its tribal societies can provide a positive model of cohesion and of cooperation for the western world — a realisation of that 'just society', based on the conciliation of its members' demands, that Mitchison had sought for a long time ("my place imagined over half a century, now real"[34], she announced in *Return to the Fairy Hill*). Mitchison's firm rejection of the conventional literary image of Africa, her grounding her fiction in the contemporary political and social reality of a continent long identified with Europe's mythical 'heart of darkness' are in themselves quite innovative. Her *Images of*

Africa (1980) — a collection of tales borrowed and adapted from stories "based on actual happenings or imagined happenings of today"[35] — are presented as the outcome of an active collaboration between the author and her Botswana friends ("Some have passed the test of reading aloud and being told that, yes you have got it right, or even, yes, how did you know?"[36]) and are addressed to a double audience, European and African, with the intent of building a sympathetic contact, "not between reason and reason, not in terms of economics or politics, but in the deeper level of the imagination"[37].

Interestingly, the collection marks also a move in Mitchison's writing from narrowly regional/national concerns to an ideal of 'cosmic' harmony and brotherhood/sisterhood. The first of her African tales ushers the reader into such vision — the first step towards mutual understanding:

> In my dream I was my father. Or did my father dream me, so that I am my father's dream? And she answered: In my dream I was my mother. If my mother dreamed me, she must have also dreamed you, since we are one.[38]

As Mitchison says — "If this bridge may be crossed, others may be built"[39]

References

1   Henry Mackenzie, *The Man of Feeling*, New York: Norton, 1958, p.72.

2   See the catalogue: *The Tiger and the Thistle. Tipu Sultan and the Scots in India 1760-1800*, Edinburgh: National Gallery of Scotland, 1999.

3   H.J.C. Grierson (ed.), *The Letters of Sir Walter Scott 1819-1821*, London: Constable, 1934, Vol.VI. p, 489 (to Lord Montagu, 1st July 1821).

4   Walter Scott, *St. Ronan's Well*, London: John C. Nimmo, 1894, Vol.II, p.173.

5   Arthur H. Williamson, "George Buchanan, Civic Virtue and Commerce: European Imperialism and its Sixteenth-Century Critics", in *The Scottish Historical Review*, Vol.LXXV, 1, No.199, 1996, pp.21-23.

6   David Hume, "Of National Characters", in *The Philosophical Works of David Hume*, Boston: Adam and Charles Black, 1854, footnote pp.228-229.

7   *Fraser's Magazine*, December 1849. Later published as pamphlet in London, in 1853. The quotation is from: *The Works of Thomas Carlyle: Critical and Miscellaneous Essays*, London: Chapman and Hall, 1899, Vol.4, pp.378-379.

8   Walter Scott, *Count Robert of Paris and The Surgeon's Daughter*, London: C. Nimmo, 1894, Vol.II, p.248.

9   Ibid., p.249.

10   R.L. Stevenson, *Vailima Letters. To Sidney Colvin 1890-1894*, London: Methuen, 1895, p.109 (24th October 1921).

11   George Blake, *Barrie and the Kailyard School*, London: Arthur Barker, 1951, p.16.

12   Robert Louis Stevenson, *Letters*, London: William Heinemann, 1926, Vol.IV, p.155 (to Henry James, December 5th 1892).

13   See Ian Campbell, *Kailyard*, Edinburgh: Ramsay Head Press, 1981.

14   J.M. Barrie, *A Window in Thrums*, London: Hodder and Stoughton, 1929, pp.8-9.

15   Cook, Richard, "The Home-Ly Kailyard Nation: Nineteenth-Century Narratives of the Highland and the Myth of Merrie Auld Scotland", in *ELH*, 1999 Winter, Vol.66, No.4, pp.1053-1073.

16   Alasdair Cameron, Adrienne Scullion, "W.F. Frame and the Scottish Popular Theatre Tradition", in Alasdair Cameron, Adrienne Scullion (eds.), *Scottish Popular Theatre and Entertainment* Glasgow: Glasgow University Library Studies, 1996, p.39.

17   David Goldie, "'Will ye stop yer tickling, Jock?': Modern and Postmodern Scottish Comedy", in *Critical Quarterly*, Vol.42, No.4, 2000, pp.7-18.

18   Maloney, Paul, "Patriotism, Empire and the Glasgow Music Hall", in *Scotlands*, 5.1, 1998, p.68.

19   Alasdair Cameron, Adrienne Scullion, "W.F. Frame and the Scottish Popular Theatre Tradition", in Alasdair Cameron, Adrienne Scullion (eds.), *Scottish Popular Theatre and Entertainment* Glasgow: Glasgow University Library Studies, 1996, pp.39-61.

20   Craig Beveridge, Ronald Turnbull, *The Eclipse of Scottish Culture. Inferiorism and the Intellectuals*, Edinburgh: Polygon, 1989.

21   Richard Gale, "Archibald MacLaren's *The Negro Slaves* and the Scottish Response to British Colonialism", in *Theatre Survey. The Journal of the American Society for Theatre Research*, Vol.35, No.2, 1994, p.84.

22   *The Negro Slaves, A Dramatic Piece, Of One Act, With Songs, Performed By His Majesty's Servants, Of The Theatre Royal, Edinburgh, Being The Original Of The Blackman And Blackbird, Performed At The Amphiteatre, Westminster Bridge*. London: 1799.

23   *Missionary Record of the United Presbyterian Church*, 2nd October 1871, New Series, Vol.4, No.LXX, pp.650-654, quoted in William, Donovan (ed.), *The Journal and Selected Writings of The Reverend Tiyo Soga*, Cape Town: A.A. Balkema, 1983, p.148.

24   Donovan Williams, *A Biography of Tiyo Soga 1829-1871*, Lovedale: Lovedale Press, 1978, p.25.

25   Letter to Sidney Colvin (10th September, 1894), in *The Letters of Robert Louis Stevenson*, Tusitala Edition, Vol.35, London: Heinemann, 1924, p.161.

26   R.L. Stevenson, *In the South Seas*, London: William Heinemann, 1925, Vol.XVIII, pp.12-13.

27   R.L. Stevenson, *Vailima Letters. To Sidney Colvin 1890-1894*, London: Methuen, 1895, p.109 (24th October 1921).

28   Ibid., p.128 (January 1st 1892).

29   From Mary Slessor, Duke Town, Calabar, To "My very dear Maggie" (17th April 1877), in *Mary Slessor: Correspondence*, Dundee: Archive and Record Centre, 1986, p.2. Transcriptions held at the National Library of Scotland.

30   Cheryl McEwan, "'The Mother of all the Peoples': geographical knowledge and the empowering of Mary Slessor", in Morag Bell, Robin Butlin, Michael Hefferman (eds.), *Geography and Imperialism 1820-1940*, Manchester: Manchester University Press, 1995, p.139.

31   W.P. Livingstone, "Old Calabar: in memory and in vision", *Free Church Record*, 1915, pp.101-108. Quoted in ibid.

32   Naomi Mitchison, *Images of Africa*, Edinburgh: Canongate, 1980, p.iii.

33   Naomi Mitchison, *The Africans: a History*, London: Panther, 1971, p.207.

34   Naomi Mitchison, *Return to the Fairy Hill*, London: Heinemann, 1966, p.52.

35   Naomi Mitchison, *Images of Africa*, Edinburgh: Canongate, 1980, p.iii.

36   Ibid.

37   Ibid.

38   Naomi Mitchison, "Images of Botswana", ibid., p.1.

39   Naomi Mitchison, *Images of Africa*, Edinburgh: Canongate, 1980, p.iii.

SIX

Vernacular Cosmopolitans:
the politics of the 'Scottish Renaissance'.

> — *Persecution, says he, all the history of the world is full of it. Perpetuating national hatred among nations.*
> — *But do you know what a nation means? says John Wyse.*
> — *Yes, says Bloom.* — *What is it? says John Wyse.*
> — *A nation? says Bloom. A nation is the same people living in the same place. [...]*
>
> James Joyce (*Ulysses*, 1922)

All attempts to re-read the past are aimed at telling our present and shaping our future. If the Union had triggered such a process, leading to the invention of a British and imperial Scottish tradition, the traumatic economic and social changes following the 1st World War, and the (implied) failure of the future imagined by previous generations of Scottish writers, originated a no less drastic revision of the idea of Scottishness — a revision that led many intellectuals and writers to see a marked watershed separating their artistic aspirations from those of the earlier century. Blake's pitilessly generalised dismissal of 19th-century Scottish fiction as a colonial and stereotyped representation of Scotland is a good example of a widespread stance:

> The bulk of Scottish fiction during the XIXth century thus fell into either of two categories: the domestic or parochial on the one hand, the romantic on the other. [...] The Scots storyteller either followed Scott and Stevenson through heather with a claymore at his belt, or he lingered round the bonnie brier bush, telling sweet amusing little stories of bucolic intrigue as seen through the windows of the Presbyterian manse. [1]

Blake phrases this sharp judgement in 1951 — by now the 'Scottish Renaissance' has become a well-established movement, and the ideas of its charismatic leader, Hugh MacDiarmid, have taken root in the Scottish *intelligentsia*. His influence on an aesthetic and ideological level will be deeply felt by successive generations of Scottish writers and critics, until at least the 1980s: an extremely valuable but also a cumbersome and contradictory legacy, in many respects, as we shall see.

It should be pointed out that the 'Renaissance' has been and remains very little explored outside Scotland. With the notable exception of MacDiarmid, its writers are still virtually unknown to the majority of readers and critics abroad. The reasons for this invisibility are several — the crystallisation of the canon of 'English literature' around the 1960s, at a time when England was firmly at the 'centre' of the UK, certainly contributed in a very large measure to their marginalisation, perpetuated in the following decades by unimaginatively standardised academic curricula around the world. Excluded from the histories and anthologies of 'English literature', they were never able to capture fully the attention of those critics who, starting from the 1980s, increasingly directed their energies towards the 'de-centring' of the literary canon, in the light of the re-evaluation of the 'margins' of the English-speaking world, especially the ex-colonies or migrant communities. Scotland was left out of this process of redefinition of the English canon, as its status lacked a definition — it could not be regarded as 'post-colonial', as it had never claimed the status of (internal) colony, and, for many, it was not even classifiable as a 'minority culture', as it had never engaged in an open struggle with the 'centre', unlike other suppressed nations, such as Ireland, Catalonia, or the Basque country. The isolation in which the writers of the 'Renaissance' operated was remarkable, and their history of neglect is hardly surprising in this context.

Isolation led to a markedly self-reflexive critical approach to this movement, whose discussion, with a few exceptions, was mainly confined to Scottish writers and scholars, well into the

1980s. Criticism between the 1960s and 1980s, in particular, proceeded along a somewhat narrow-minded track, focussing mainly on a few charismatic (eminently male) figures, and on Hugh MacDiarmid's work and entourage. A remarkable exclusion was represented by the many women who were active both as writers and as promoters of the Renaissance. Their contribution was often downrated by their male colleagues, and literary historians followed passively in their footsteps, so that their names — until very recent times — appeared mainly as a footnote to histories of Scottish literature. Lewis Grassic Gibbon, for example, in his iconoclastic "Literary Lights", denies Naomi Mitchison, Willa Muir and Catherine Carswell the status of Scottish writers. They are in good company, no doubt, as Gibbon bans from the Scottish canon all those who do not write either in Scots or Gaelic (obviously siding with Muir, who believed that there can be no national literature where there is no national language). Yet, the exclusion of three of the most established Renaissance women is striking. Of Mitchison for example, the only woman writer he seems to value as a novelist, he claims:

> She is the one writer of 'historical' novels in modern English who commands respect and enthusiasm. Her pages are aglow with a fine essence of apprehended light. *The Conquered* and *Black Sparta* light up the human spirit very vividly and truly. And they are in no sense Scots books though written by a Scots-woman.[2]

It is with similar words that MacDiarmid dismisses Carswell's semi-autobiographical novel, set between her native Glasgow and London, *Open the Door!* (1920), as "a deft but superficial study in personalities"[3]. A strikingly elusive comment for a novel — published in London and awarded the Melrose Prize in 1920 — which offers a powerful evocation of Glasgow at the turn the century, as well as an interesting portrait of the artist as a young (Scots)woman. In general women writers have been regarded as unable to articulate or represent Scottishness effectively because — as in the above comments — they are seen as too keen on the representation of 'human nature' and 'personality' to be able to apprehend the larger whole of the nation. They tend to be appreciated (if at all) as 'networkers' and supporters of the movement, rather than active and creative members — as is the case with Helen B. Cruickshank (to whom Hugh MacDiarmid and Lewis Grassic Gibbon dedicate jointly with "affection and admiration" their *Scottish Scene* in 1934), a poet and a writer, but mainly remembered as a tireless hostess and organiser of events. A 'mother' rather than a protagonist.

It is somewhat beyond the scope of the present chapter to re-assess systematically the Renaissance, yet there is no doubt that such re-appraisal is today very much needed. A wider and more inclusive outlook would undoubtedly lead to a better understanding of this crucial chapter in Scotland's cultural and literary history and to a better and broader contextualisation of its production. Critics have, for example, often maintained that "there is indeed much in Scottish writing to indicate that the city has not yet been fully assimilated into the psychological framework of many Scots people" [4]. Muir's or Gibbon's words of horror and revulsion at the sight of Glasgow slums can only confirm this assumption:

> . . . the crumbling houses, the twisted faces, the obscene words casually heard in passing, the ancient haunting stench of pollution and decay, the arrogant women, the mean men, the terrible children, daunted me, and at last filled me with an immense, blind dejection. [5]

> In Glasgow there are over a hundred and fifty thousand human beings [...]. The hundred and fifty thousand eat and sleep and copulate and conceive and crawl into childhood in those waste jungles of stench and disease and hopelessness, sub-humans as definitely as the Morlocks of Wells . . . . [6]

Catherine Carswell — ignored by critics until very recent times — provides an antithetical view of the same industrialised metropolis. Born in Glasgow into a well-to-do merchant family, she articulates a participation in and a fascination with all the diverse layers and facets of her home town, including that life of the lower classes that had deeply unsettled her male colleagues.

Her portrait of Glasgow reveals an author who has not only fully assimilated the city, but even revels in its fluid and composite nature:

> . . . in the teeming Saturday night crowd, where all the men and women, and even children at the breast, were openly drunk, drunkenness assumed an epic quality. It was an orgy, an abandon, a bacchanal, a celebration, a wild defiance. Shawled women fought, screaming and tearing each other's hair, while the men stood round roaring them on with laughter. . . The spectacle was shocking. But it had a sordid splendour, a whole-hearted, ruinous contempt which, for the moment, excluded other considerations . . . [7]

As an honorary secretary, networker and factotum of the newly founded Scottish P.E.N. ("Certainly I felt I was living about four or five lives in one"[8], she explained), Helen B. Cruickshank was able to describe with realistic lucidity the changes taking place on the Scottish cultural and literary scene in the period between the wars – her minimalist style and inclusive outlook counterbalances that of her friend MacDiarmid, the 'Prophet', as she affectionately nicknamed him.[9] Her evocation of the Renaissance is always suggestive of a popular movement, rather than an elite's accomplishment:

> In Scotland many felt that even in our own country there was not enough knowledge of our cultural heritage, and there is no doubt that the rising tide of national Scottish sentiment brought many members into the movement. [10]

The carefully annotated pages of her *Octobiography* (1976) record minutiae side by side with the testimony of established leaders of the movement, and never fail to stress how wide-spread the demand for a re-definition of Scottishness was, both in literary and cultural terms. The number of formal and impromptu debates, the heterogeneity of the political and social stance of the participants, shed light – in her 'domestic' report – on the extent and the character of this 'quiet revolution'.

Having said this, it cannot but be acknowledged that MacDiarmid's contribution to the development and subsequent promotion of both the Scottish P.E.N. and of the so-called 'Scottish Renaissance' was crucial and rife with pioneering ideas, and that it did indeed represent a dramatic 'point of departure' for 20th-century Scottish culture. It is necessary, then, to assess his contribution to a movement of which he was undoubtedly a 'shifting force', as aptly phrased in Seamus Heaney's lines:

> The weather-eye of a poetry like the weather,
> a shifting force, a factor factored in
> whether it prevails or not . . . [11]

MacDiarmid's main concern, we may say today, borrowing a phrase from the Kenyan writer and scholar Ngugi wa Thion'go, was that of 'decolonising the mind'[12] of the Scots, as he set as his first and foremost goal his country's creative autonomy from England, and its emancipation from the debased self-image and the widespread sense of inferiority which were the 'colonial' legacy of the Union. The definition of a new Scottish cultural identity, distinct from the supra-national, British one and also different from the 'provincial' one, which had shaped Scotland in the course of the 19th century, was then the priority of his programme. Political independence would have been a consequence, not a pre-requisite – this entailed a long process of negotiation and debate with the 'centre' rather than an abrupt divorce. That the pen did not give way to the sword, as it were, may have deprived Scotland of yet another 'romantic' chapter in its history (and also slowed down considerably the process of its cultural de-colonisation), but certainly had many positive, far-ranging consequences, as we shall see. Equally positive, at least potentially, was MacDiarmid's creation of a 'hybrid' model as the most effective means of conveying Scotland's new, reformed self-image — "the wonderful diversity and innumerable/ Sharp transitions of the Scottish Scene" [13]. His best known poem, *A Drunk Man Looks at the Thistle* (1926), is also a celebration of his country's "multifarious" and metamorphic identity — a "mongrel" identity — of its rich syncreticity and multi-layered make-up. The poem weaves a fabric which connects 'low' to 'high' culture, oral to written literary expression, Scots to English, and to several other languages, hybridising diachronic and synchronic dialects. Pastiche and contamination were techniques common to modernist texts; less common is the revelling in this hybrid dimension, which obviously characterises his work. Not only did MacDiarmid's idea of a Scottish 'mongrel' identity provide an effective interpretative model for his country's culture (a model which, in recent years, has been fully re-evaluated, with a renewed emphasis on Scotland's polyphonic and pluralistic tradition), but it also allowed him to distance himself from those contemporary European expressions of nationalism, which, in the 1920s and 1930s, grounded themselves in ideals of cohesive, fixed and exclusive national features — language, history, tradition and, very often, race.

That Scotland in the 20th century was gradually coming to regard itself as an 'internal colony' or as a 'minority culture' within the United Kingdom, was not, in itself, a guarantee that it would not follow in the ideological footsteps of those nation-states, or 'majority cultures' — England, in this case — whose political and cultural ascendancy it was set on challenging. In fact, in many 20th-century anti-imperial movements the construction of a fixed and monolithic national culture, markedly distinct from the dominant one, but ultimately structured on the same 'exclusive' ideology, seemed to be the first, inevitable step on the road to independence. Recently, this antagonistic phase of many an irredentist movement, has been described as both "insufficient and crucial" by Edward Said — crucial in order to raise anti-colonial resentment, insufficient for the narrowness of the constructions of national identity which stem from it, stifled as they are by a strong conflicting impulse and an 'anxiety of difference', an outright fear of not being 'different enough' from the dominant culture.[14] This phase of entrenched 'negative dialectics' with the centre may be inevitable, but it certainly comes at a cost, as these rigid constructions are extraordinarily tenacious. Difference — emphasised through a series of 'essential' features such as language, religious affiliation, ethnicity or racial attributes, then becomes a set of norms outside which nationhood cannot be claimed. In other words, what is originally a 'description' of a culture becomes a prescriptive model, to the (potential) detriment of other 'minorities', in what seems to establish itself as an endless, vicious cycle. It is precisely this phase of 'monocular', entrenched nationalism that James Joyce openly attacks in "Cyclops", the episode of Ulysses where Leopold Bloom is faced by the wrath of the 'citizen', the 'one-eyed' supporter of the cause of Irish independence, locked into a ferociously anti-English view, repudiating all that he regards as extraneous to the 'pure' Irish tradition — from the hybridised Anglo-Irish culture of many Dubliners to Bloom's Jewishness. It is Bloom's embodiment of a non-Catholic Irishness, and his reminding the citizen that the Jesus worshipped by Christians was a Jew that, by destabilising the rigidly codified categories defended by the 'cyclop', makes his blind (and somewhat helpless) fury explode. Any idea of 'Irishness' in fact — as implied by Joyce — is inextricably linked to that 'Other' that the citizen attempts to exclude from the representation of his culture. His anxiety of difference gradually and inevitably develops into abuse and physical violence as he assaults Bloom, at the end of the episode. Joyce was far from putting into question Ireland's demand for independence, which he supported whole-heartedly, rather, he aimed at denouncing the flaws in the brand of nationalism which, in that particular historical period, was at the forefront of the Home Rule battle.

Scotland and Ireland share a similar, but certainly not identical history and relation to England. As James Barke claimed, in a special issue of the *Left Review* (1936) dedicated to the Scottish question:

> The overwhelming majority of the Scottish people do not feel that they are suffering from the oppression of a conquering nation. Unlike certain sections of the Irish people, they do not feel that they are a subject race forced to submit to an alien domination. [15]

Barke, like many Scottish left-wing writers in this period, was not and could not be insensitive to the 'national question', even though his main concern was the political reform of society along the lines of the Socialist International. His idea that the Scots did have a distinct tradition and cultural identity, but were not looking for political independence as they were not 'oppressed' by England, was in fact shared by many of his contemporaries, some of whom went to the extent of regretting, quite paradoxically, this state of things. As Edwin Muir put it: "The unfortunate thing for Scotland is that it is not an obviously oppressed nation, as Ireland was, but only a depressed one, searching for the source of its depression"[16]. The implication of Muir's remark is quite obvious: without a 'real' repression there cannot be a 'real' nationalism. And Scotland was doomed to disappear. Yet, it is this very 'failure', largely determined by Scotland's anomalous predicament (attributable, for some, to the Scots' incapacity to antagonise the English unconditionally), that encouraged the development of a conception of nationhood quite independent from the 'negative dialectics' (that is from a definition that is strictly grounded on negative scrutiny) that dominate the discourse of the nation in the early 20th century.

In what way, and why then, did the Scottish Renaissance differ from other movements which were also fostering cultural independence at about the same time in the waning British Empire? The cardinal assumption was undoubtedly the same everywhere: the need for a re-definition of the native culture and for its emancipation from the Anglocentric model. Hugh MacDiarmid, for example, often lamented Scotland's inability to resist England's centralising tendency, and launched a campaign for its de-provincialisation:

> The tendency inherent in the Union, to assimilate Scotland to England, and ultimately to provincialise the former . . . has, as a matter of fact, not yet been effectively countered by the emergence of any principle demanding a reversed tendency. [17]

He was not the only one to denounce this sorrowful plight and to advocate a rebirth of national culture. In a series of letters, published in David Cleghorn Thomson's *Scotland in Quest of her Youth* (1932), some of the most distinguished writers of the period including Eric Linklater, Naomi Mitchison and Neil M. Gunn, articulate in similar words the same concern about Scotland's future. Interestingly, they all seem to agree on the fact that the term 'Renaissance' — by now a current one — does not refer to the present state of things, but rather describes a project of renewal, located in a vague time to be, whose success is still deemed uncertain. According to George Blake, for example, "It may mean that Scotland is going to enjoy a fruitful renaissance. On the other hand, it may not."[18] James Bridie sounds decidedly more pessimistic and dismissive: "You must excuse me from writing about them till they show the stamina and consistency of output of Scots engineers, or pathologists or philosophers or chemists" [19]. The reader who is unfamiliar with this movement and its history will be struck by the contrast between its promising name and its representatives' attitude — certainly not what one would describe as positive or self-confident. At a later date, Cruickshank's retrospective evaluation of the movement does not alter much the impressions of her colleagues in the 1930s:

> In public I have always been careful to call this literary movement "the so-called Scottish Renaissance", for, despite the undoubted quickening of the literary life of Scotland during the last forty years, I have never been able to persuade myself that it merited this somewhat grandiose title. [20]

In general, then, we could say that there is expectancy and a strong sense of commitment, but not the blind determination that fosters an armed rebellion, as it were. There is also a remarkable attention towards the definition of a 'national literature', whose shape and constituents are not taken for granted — yet another sign that at least this generation of Scottish intellectuals did not rely on a pre-set model. Catherine Carswell provides one of its most interesting 'negative' definitions, adopting a perspective that James Joyce might well have approved of:

Possibly some of our best Scottish writers to come, while they will see the world through Scottish eyes and with full Scottish acknowledgements, will not wish to write about Scotland, at all. They may desire more naturally to write about Russia . . ., or about Canada, or even about London. . . . In this way, as in some others, we resemble the Jews. Our eyes turn ever outwards from our homes and our feet carry us to many lands. What we need is a new significance in that home from which we so readily stray. [21]

The likening of the Scots to the Jews, and thus to a people who would not define themselves in closed territorial terms, and her reference to a 'nomadic' dimension of Scottishness point towards a definition of identity which is dynamic, transnational and 'open'. Euro-American modernists — ex-pats and 'exiles' — in the same period when Carswell is writing these lines, promote an idea of national identity which matters only in its distance from a present space and time. Carswell, born at the turn of the century in Scotland, educated in Glasgow and Frankfurt, a freelance journalist and a biographer who lived in London and in England most of her adult life, shared with the modernists (many of whom were her friends) a similar lifestyle and culture, but, as a Scotswoman, she could not and would not give up the 'here and now' — the 'local', was still a relevant element in her personal experience as well as in her literary vision. The same can be said of Hugh MacDiarmid and Lewis Grassic Gibbon. The latter had been particularly straightforward in his appeal to transcend nationalism and — quite prophetically — had foreseen the threat of closure and fundamentalism posed by 'small' nations:

What a curse to the earth are small nations! Latvia, Lithuania, Poland, Finland, San Salvador, Luxembourg, Manchuko, the Irish Free State . . . A time will come when nationalism, with other cultural aberrations, will have passed from the human spirit, when Man, again free and unchained, has all the earth for his footstool, sings his epics in a language moulded from the best on earth [...] I am a nationalist only in the sense that the sane Heptarchian was a Wessexman or a Mercian or what not: temporarily, opportunistically. I think the Braid Scots may yet give lovely lights and shadows not only to English but to the perfected speech of Cosmopolitan Man: so I cultivate it, for lack of that perfect speech that is yet to be. [22]

How could a Renaissance writer, an intellectual who was committing himself to the 'rebirth' of Scotland attack the very ideology that — in the eyes of many Scottish scholars of the generations to come — he should have embraced and promoted? This passage has often been downplayed as an eccentric expression of an author who had an iconoclastic and 'ferocious' style of argumentation, even though there is ample evidence, in his fiction, that this 'cosmopolitan' view was crucial to him at least as much as the 'local' (Scottish) one. A close reading of his best-known work — A Scots Quair — will reveal the presence of both pulls, centripetal and centrifugal, and also an attempt to balance them. Gibbon has since been, questionably, assimilated to the traditionally nationalistic stance often attributed to the intellectuals at work in this period. What he and his contemporaries were articulating (often unwittingly) was an attempt to re-formulate the very idea of national identity: rather than bending Scottishness to fit into current models of anti-imperial nationalism, or to merge with the 'centre', or to yield to the internationalist appeal of Socialism, they tried to forge a model which could accommodate the complexity of their experience. Just like MacDiarmid, Gibbon committed himself to the shaping of a new literary language to express his sense of belonging, coining what we could describe as a brand of 'vernacular cosmopolitanism' — an attempt to ally what were then seen as two irreconcilable perspectives, that is the wish to be a citizen with full rights of the global Cosmopolis and yet maintain a proud 'provincial' standpoint.

In recent years, geopolitics has sought to investigate "the irredeemable plurality of space and the multiplicity of possible political constructions of space"[23] and has provided a mode of representation adequate to post-modern times, by fusing the two traditionally polarised dimensions — global/local — into the 'glocalised' web of complex economic and cultural relations that organise our life, [24] beyond the conventional forms of (geo)political organisation. As one of the leading theorists in this field of studies has claimed, "glocalization . . . can implode geopolitics"[25], as it is bound to erode our inherited imagination of a world organised in spatial blocs and fixed identities. It is not far-fetched to claim that the work of writers like MacDiarmid and Gibbon tended — unwittingly — rather to problematise and unsettle the conventional practices of nationhood, and to define new 'categories', than to follow in the ready-made footsteps of traditional definitions. Their 'vernacular cosmopolitanism' can be regarded as a first, perhaps raw attempt to tell the 'glocal'.

It has to be stressed that their quest was not an easy one, and its outcome was not always homogeneous or persuasive: the Renaissance writers lacked the conceptual and methodological tools to carry out their reform and, as already stated, they worked in isolation. The iconoclastic and 'eccentric' style, for example, often characterises the works of MacDiarmid and Gibbon and made their reception beyond Scottish borders often problematic (it is almost impossible to integrate them into the established literary and cultural movements of the period), can certainly be explained by the limitations placed on their experimentation by contemporary ideological and cultural tendencies. It is interesting, in this respect, and of some significance, that most of the writers of the first generation of the Scottish Renaissance distanced themselves not only from the cultural and ideological stance of the 'centre', but also from contemporary expressions of Irish nationalism, like Gibbon, in "Glasgow", or like Carswell, who advocated a similarly distinct approach, albeit more diplomatically:

> We are still feeling our way. Let us be allowed to feel it. Let us remember that we are — among other things — truly a nation of critics, and permit us to be self-critical as befits our nature. One of the greatest mistakes we can make is to think in any renaissance of our own we can follow in the footsteps of the Irish. We are utterly different from the Irish.[26]

MacDiarmid also stressed the substantial difference between the Irish and Scottish projects and made an interesting prophecy:

> ... the Scottish psychology differs from the Irish, and, nationalistically laggard as Scotland has been in comparison with other countries, there are grounds for anticipating that, once it does waken up, it will redeem the leeway at a single stride and be the first to penetrate into that arcanum which still foils even Mr de Valera with its intangible and ubiquitous barriers. [27]

While today we cannot subscribe to MacDiarmid's idea of an 'essential' Scottish psychology (this is just one of the many examples of how he and his colleagues 'stumble' into terms and images belonging to a traditionally nationalistic ideology) we are nonetheless struck by his idea that Scotland is going to find a 'new way', as it were, beyond current practices of nationhood. Significantly, while he envisages the possibility of a revolution in this field, he falls short of describing it. The time is not ripe yet.

That the re-definition of Scottishness entailed a 'revolution' in thinking and not simply a redress of wrongs or a re-establishment of ancient cultural/political borders is a belief shared also by Catherine Carswell. In an article published in 1936 she reminds her readers that

> The makers of the great encyclopaedias of the past were poets, heretics and innovators who were animated by a desire that transcended, while it also included the imparting of knowledge... That is to say, the encyclopedists who have mattered have been fighters before they were compilers, because they were faced with the compilation of dangerous material. [28]

An encyclopaedia can be a means of propaganda, and as such, it can propagate a "new world of revolutionary knowledge"[29], and thus have — like the 9th edition of the *Encyclopedia Britannica*, by a Scotsman, Robertson Smith — a great impact on society. Or it can become "a dead thing", a commercial enterprise subject to the demands of publishers and the establishment. Smith — according to Carswell the last of a line of innovative compilers of encyclopaedias — had been predictably "attacked in Scotland as an atheist"[30], where he was obviously perceived as a danger to the status quo. And yet Scotland, with its rich and long-standing experience in this field — Carswell contends — can go back to the true spirit of this potentially revolutionary institution and give the world an 'encyclopedia scotica' — "a 'new plan', even though this would bring down the fulminations that were showered upon Diderot and Robertson Smith"[31]. It is this new revolutionary knowledge which — according to Carswell — alone can lead to a 'Renaissance' worthy of the name[32].

If on one side MacDiarmid and his contemporaries could not fully identify with the 'negative dialectics' of contemporary expressions of nationalism, on the other they had to deal with the powerful and pervasive construction of the 'centre' of the time — namely with T.S. Eliot's essentialist definition of national tradition, and with his insistence on principles — like continuity and organicity — that were bound to marginalise Scotland and all those cultures which could not boast an ancient and (assumedly) uninterrupted line of development. As Cairns Craig has pointed out, the ideas developed by Eliot on this subject became open indictment in his notorious "Was there a Scottish literature?"[33] (1919), where he isolated "five or six (at most) great organic formations of history", that is traditions whose value was established and 'universal'. Other traditions and histories, outside these, did of course exist, according to Eliot, but they would bear a strictly local (i.e. negligible) relevance[34]. This is of course only one step ahead of Matthew Arnold's views on Burns and Scottish poetry ("The real Burns is of course in his Scotch poems . . ."[35]) as a phenomenon of purely 'regional' relevance. Scottish writers could choose whether they should yield their national identity and merge into a 'real', organic tradition, or remain 'local' and thus consign their work to oblivion.

MacDiarmid's work can of course be read as a response and a challenge to Eliot's theories — speaking, as he was, from "whaur extremes meet", and trying to articulate a vision of nationhood beyond current theorisations. His work is inevitably rife with tensions and contradictions, as well as with brave attempts to appropriate the discourse of the nation. His famous motto, for example, coined for *The Scottish Chapbook* ("Not Traditions — Precedents"), can be seen in this context as an attempt to subvert Eliot's cardinal requirement for an organic and unified literary and linguistic practice, and to claim a dignified status for Scottish or for any 'minor' literature. In MacDiarmid's vision the margins could indeed 'write back to the centre' and thus contribute to a broader-based re-definition of tradition. In "English Ascendancy in British Literature" (1931) he foresees the establishment of such a wider *koine* — quite ahead of his time:

> It is absurd that the intelligent reader of English, who would be ashamed not to know something (if only the leading names, and roughly, what they stand for) of most Continental literatures, is content to ignore Scottish, Irish and Welsh Gaelic literatures, and Scots Vernacular literature. . . . Few literatures offer within themselves so rich a range of alterative values, of material for comparative criticism, as does, not English, but British, meaning by the latter that common culture . . . which includes not only English (and English dialect) literature, but the Gaelic and Scots Vernacular literatures as well.[36]

Another outstanding writer of this period, not endowed with the same prophetic and imaginative powers as MacDiarmid—Edwin Muir — was faced by the same inherent contradictions and succumbed to them, encountering fierce opposition from his friend. MacDiarmid never forgave Muir's 'defeatism', yet Muir's analysis of the anomalous predicament of the Scottish writer, even though imbued with pessimism, is in many ways more lucid and often more accessible than that offered by MacDiarmid himself. Scotland's 'isolation' and the lack of adequate interpretative models for its predicament are central issues in many of his writings. Scotland — he explained — was living in a condition of "unchanging suspended potentiality", "half within the world of life and half outside it":

Scotland has not become a real part of England, nor has it succeeded in remaining a separate and independent entity. That is the problem. All that effectively remains out of it, therefore, is a name and an aspiration which, until recently, has never seriously wished to be fulfilled. [37]

This, in fact, is quite an honest and realistic statement: Scotland is a 'suspended' country in this historical period and there are no ready-made, suitable definitions for its predicament. Muir is not a visionary, he is not a 'prophet' — he simply makes use of to the descriptive and ideological tools that are available to him. He cannot but acknowledge the death of Scottish culture. His pessimism is infectious. Unable to pick up and transmit the most innovative and progressive ideas developed by some of the first generation 'Renaissance' writers, subsequent generations of Scottish writers and critics seemed to lapse back into traditional expressions of nationalism, which, quite inevitably, triggered the widespread, deep sense of frustration and failure that surfaces in much Scottish literature between the 1960s and the 1980s.

Reasons for this 'failure' — as most Scottish readers will know, unlike most non-Scottish ones — have been sought for and found in the gradual de-nationalisation of post-Union Scotland, in the adoption of Protestantism and the consequent close links with England, in the degradation to the status of dialects of the native languages (Scots and Gaelic), in the end or the interruption of a continuous national literary tradition marked by the Union. It is quite appropriate to state, as Valentina Poggi does with reference to Fionn MacColla, that the work of many Scottish writers in this historical period is "based on a lifelong quarrel with history"[38]. Scots' self-hatred for having been severed from their past and for not being able to stand up against England, for being 'out of history' becomes a *leitmotiv* in the second half of the 20th century — at times even a mannerism, as in Irvine Welsh's *Trainspotting* (1993), when one of the 'junkies' (famously) remarks:

It's nae good blamin it oan the English fir colonising us. Ah don't hate the English. They're just wankers. We are colonised by wankers. We

can't even pick a decent, vibrant, healthy culture to be colonised by.
No. We're ruled by effete arseholes. What does that make us? The
lowest of the fuckin low, the scum of the earth. . . . Ah don't hate the
English. They just git oan wi the shite thuv goat. Ah hate the Scots. [39]

Less transgressive than the use of demotic language seems to
imply, the passage provides a concentration of commonplaces
regarding the state of things in the Scottish nation. In fact, it can
be said to go back to Muir's disconsolate statement that "The
unfortunate thing for Scotland is that it is not an obviously
oppressed nation, as Ireland was. . ."[40], and, more generally, to the
rooted Scottish regret for the absence of a strong 'negative dialectics'
with the 'centre'. It also summarises what can be considered as the
negative legacy (or the degeneration) of the Renaissance — a strong
emphasis on social realism (with the subsequent exclusion of other
modes) and a tendency to identify Scottishness with the working-
class. William McIlvanney's novels, for example, where national
identity is made to coincide with the sense of brotherhood and
solidarity that binds workers (and is therefore deeply inflected by
gender), are certainly close to what we could define as an
'essentialist' vision of nationhood. The critique of capitalism and
the strong focus on the working classes find ample justification in
Scotland's post-war economic and social crisis, yet, their emphasis
has been undeniably detrimental to a wider articulation of
Scottishness. The narrowing down of the terms defining Scottish
literature can be seen at work quite early in the 20th century, for
example in Fionn MacColla's indictment of Lewis Grassic Gibbon's
free interpretation of the ancient history of his native Mearns:

. . . those "happy Maglemosians" of his "without priest or king" who
apparently did no work or who didn't find the soil of the Mearns
grudging and parsimonious — all this aspect of his writing is simply
deplorable: worse — since we are talking of truth — downright
irresponsible. We are a nation which has slowly died because of a lie
in the mind and the will; in whose case, therefore, there is a desperate
need for truth and strict accuracy, for well-considered, well-based
judgements about our past.[41]

'Realism' — supposedly an antidote for the 'false' representations of imperial Scotland — soon becomes a poison. The censorious tone of MacColla here is but one example. The Scottish literary canon, gradually defined between the 1960s and the 1980s, constructed as it is in antithesis with the 'centre', and in utter isolation from the international literary debate, is marked by inexplicable omissions and 'sidelines'. Writers who have reached fame outside Scotland are frequently neglected at home: James Macpherson/Ossian remains the most notable exclusion, while 19th-century novelists are — as we have seen — generally downrated for their insufficient adherence to 'reality'. Edwin Muir, undoubtedly the single case of a Scottish poet celebrated in Europe as well as in the USA in the 20th-century, is marginalised at home, so much so that he chooses exile. This resulted — quite literally — in a short circuit in communication with the 'external world', further exacerbated, at times, by the 'Anglophobic' stance adopted by some writers and literary critics, who strove to enhance whatever was distinctively 'native' as opposed to what was perceived as a specifically English heritage. It goes without saying that the interaction and exchange between English and Scottish writers has been intensely fruitful, since the Middle Ages, and to discard it or ignore it means to deprive both literatures of a major interpretative key. There are networks of reciprocal making that bind Scotland's literary tradition to Europe, North America and the rest of the world — but those connecting it to England have to be privileged, for obvious historical reasons.

Difficult (and hazardous) as it is to generalise, it can be argued that the 'Scottish Renaissance', in the period between the wars, contained the germs of a conception of nationhood which was different from the 'Cyclopic' model of nationalism current then in Europe, and much closer to the late 20th- century redefinition of nation. These germs were largely neglected by later generations, to surface again, gradually, in the renewed political and cultural atmosphere of the late 1980s and 1990s. Alasdair Gray, for example, one of Scotland's most established and original contemporary novelists, does not share the widespread pessimism about the bleak future of Scotland He has developed a distinctly fantastic-realistic mode of narration and has significantly retrieved Hugh MacDiarmid's metamorphic symbol of Scotland — the *Drunk Man's Thistle* — by re-writing his famous poem into a novel. *1982 Janine* (1984) takes us on a 24-hour journey through the consciousness of a middle-aged, alcoholic failure, showing how he is eventually able to piece together his shattered self into a new, precarious and yet joyous identity. Jock, at the end of the novel, epitomises his country, coming to terms with his past mistakes and shaping his future, optimistically, out of them:

> I will stand on the platform an hour from now, briefcase in hand, a neater figure than most but not remarkable. I will have the poise of an acrobat to step on to a high wire, of an actor about to take the stage in a wholly new play. Nobody will guess what I am going to do. I do not know it myself. But I will not do nothing. No, I will not do nothing.[42]

References

1   George, Blake, *Barrie and the Kailyard School*, London: Arthur Barker, 1951, pp.12-13.

2   Lewis Grassic Gibbon, "Literary Lights", in Lewis Grassic Gibbon, Hugh MacDiarmid, *Scottish Scene: or the Intelligent Man's Guide to Albyn*, London: Jarrolds, 1934, p.168.

3   Hugh MacDiarmid, "Newer Scottish Fiction (II): Others", (2.7.26), in Hugh MacDiarmid, *Contemporary Scottish Studies*, (Alan Riach ed.) Manchester: Carcanet, 1995, p.350.

4   Manfred Malzahn, *Aspects of Identity. The Contemporary Scottish Novel (1978-1981)*, Frankfurt am Main: Peter Lang, 1984, p.30.

5   Edwin Muir, *An Autobiography*, London: The Hogarth Press, 1954, pp.91-92.

6   Lewis Grassic Gibbon, "Glasgow", in Lewis Grassic Gibbon, Hugh MacDiarmid, *Scottish Scene: or the Intelligent Man's Guide to Albyn*, London: Jarrolds, 1934, p.116.

7   Catherine Carswell, "Glasgow", in *Lying Awake. An Unfinished Autobiography and Other Posthumous Papers*, Edinburgh: Canongate, 1997, p.20.

8   Helen B. Cruickshank, *Octobiography*, Montrose: Standard Press, 1976, p.75.

9   Ibid.

10 Ibid., p.68.

11 Seamus Heaney, "An Invocation: In Memoriam Hugh MacDiarmid", in *The Spirit Level*, London: Faber & Faber, 1996, p.28.

12 See Ngugi wa Thiong'o, *Decolonising the Mind. The Politics of Language in African Literature*, Oxford: James Currey, 1986.

13   Hugh MacDiarmid, "Direadh I", in *The Complete Poems of Hugh MacDiarmid*. Vol.II, Michael Grieve, W.R. Aitken (eds.), Harmondsworth: Penguin, 1985, p.1170.

14   See Paul Atkinson, *The Ethnographic Imagination*, London: Routledge, 1990, p.1.

15   James Barke, "The Scottish National Question", in *Left Review*, Vol.2, No.14, 1936, p.739.

16   Edwin Muir, *Scottish Journey*, London: Heinemann & Gollancz, 1935, p.29.

17   C.M. Grieve, *Albyn, or Scotland and the Future*, London: Kegan Paul, 1927, p.49.

18   David Cleghorn Thomson, *Scotland in Quest of Her Youth*, Edinburgh: Oliver and Boyd, 1932, p.159.

19   Ibid., p.160.

20   Helen B. Cruickshank, *Octobiography*, Montrose: Standard Press, 1976, p.77.

21   David Cleghorn Thomson, *Scotland in Quest of Her Youth*, Edinburgh: Oliver and Boyd, 1932, p.162.

22   Lewis Grassic Gibbon, "Glasgow", in Lewis Grassic Gibbon, Hugh MacDiarmid, *Scottish Scene*, London: Jarrolds, 1934, p.122 and p.124.

23   Gearóid Ó Tuathail, Simon Dalby (eds.), *Rethinking Geopolitics*, London: Routledge, 1998, p.3.

24   Tim Luke, "Placing power/siting space: The politics of global and local in the New World Order", in *Society and Space*, No.12, 1994, pp.613-628.

25   Ibid., p.629.

26   David Cleghorn Thomson, *Scotland in Quest of her Youth*, Edinburgh: Oliver and Boyd, 1932, p.161.

27   C.M. Grieve, *Albyn, or Scotland and the Future*, London: Kegan Paul, 1927, pp.94-95.

28   Catherine Carswell, "Encyclopedia Scotica", in *Left Review*, Vol.2, No.14, 1936, p.765.

29   Ibid.

30   Ibid.

31   Ibid., p.767.

32   Ibid.

33   T.S. Eliot, "Was there a Scottish Literature?", in *The Aethenaeum*, 4657, 1st August 1919, p.680.

34   Cairns Craig, "Peripheries", in *Out of History. Narrative Paradigms in Scottish and British Culture*, Edinburgh: Polygon, 1996, pp.11-30. (Originally published in *Cencrastus* No.8, 1983).

35   Matthew Arnold "The Study of Poetry" (1880), in *The Complete Works of Matthew Arnold*, Ann Arbor: The University of Michigan Press, 1973, p.182. See Chap.3.

36   Hugh MacDiarmid, "English Ascendancy in British Literature", in Hugh MacDiarmid, *Selected Prose* Alan Riach (ed.), Manchester: Carcanet, 1992, pp.67-68, 69. (Originally published in *The Criterion*, 1931).

37   Edwin Muir, "The Functionlessness of Scotland", in *Free Man*, 11th February 1935, p.6.

38   Valentina Poggi, "History and the reconstructive imagination in Fionn's MacColla's works", in *Écosse: Regards d'Histoire. Actes du Congrés international d'études écossaises, Grenoble, 1991*, Grenoble: G.D.R.Etudes écossaises, 1992, p.265.

39   Irvine Welsh, *Trainspotting*, London: Vintage, 1999, p.78.

40   Edwin Muir, *Scottish Journey*, London: Heinemann & Gollancz, 1935, p.29.

41   Fionn MacColla, *Ro Fhad Mar So A Tha Mi/ Too Long in This Condition*, Thurso: John Humphries, 1975, p.5.

42   Alasdair Gray, *1982 Janine*, Harmondsworth: Penguin, p.341.

SEVEN

"Close your eyes and imagine a Scot": a question of (in)visibility

Orientals were rarely seen or looked at: they were seen through, analysed not as citizens, or even people, but as problems to be solved or confined, or ... taken over.

Edward Said (*Orientalism*, 1991)

Now, close your eyes and imagine a German. Close your eyes and imagine, a Belgian, a Muslim, a Protestant, a Croat, a Celt, a Bosnian, a Jew, a Slav, a Pole, a Canadian, a Catholic, don't stop, the list is as endless as the human race ...

Maud Sulter ("Blood Money", 1994)

The term 'representation' has, for most of us, a neutral connotation — it stands for a 'likeness' and it has an implied visual component: someone who is 'represented' is someone who 'appears' and, therefore, who is 'present'. In fact, representations (of histories, cultures, people — in written texts, images, films, TV, oral reports) are never innocent, as recent critical theories have demonstrated. As Edward Said has observed in *Orientalism* (1978), for example, "in any instance of at least written language, there is no such thing as a delivered presence, but a re-presence, or a representation."[1]. Said refers to what he describes as "the highly artificial enactment of what a non-Oriental has made into a symbol for the whole Orient"[2] — that is the depiction of the East spread by western artists, historians and writers, especially in the course of the 19th century, which excluded the natives' perspective and experience, thus making them invisible.

A representation, then, far from being a neutral rendering of a determined 'object', is an ideological tool, which can serve various purposes, including that of sustaining a colonialist project by reinforcing systems of inequality and subordination. Literary texts, in particular, offer powerful (and often popular) representations of cultures and of individuals within their native culture — hegemonic relations between 'centre' and 'margins' can thus be shaped, strengthened or even challenged. No surprise then that the questioning of literary texts has become so crucial in addressing the predicament of the subaltern — be it a minority group, a marginalised social class, a colonised country. No surprise, either, that the debate over the status of national literature in Scotland in the past century has mainly focussed on the issue of representation, as we have seen in the previous chapters. Questions tackled by the Renaissance writers and the following generations included that of an ideologically manipulated depiction of Scotland's past and culture, or of a downright erasure of most of its relevant aspects within the United Kingdom. As Alan Riach has explained: "With the rise of the British Empire, two things happened to Scotland: it became invisible, and it became internationally recognisable in stereotypes and caricatures"[3]. Invisibility, as far as Scots were concerned, was not the outcome of a downright interdiction of self-expression (within the British Empire this applied only to slaves in the Carribean and to Highlanders in the aftermath of the second Jacobite rebellion): they were of course allowed to retain their own culture and yet, as we have seen, this was undoubtedly marginalised by the dominant Anglocentric perspective. Scots were both active and passive recipients of the view from the centre — they chose or were compelled to 'mimic' the dominant group, thus developing a complex relation with it. Even invisibility — as the present chapter purports to demonstrate — has different shades.

The fate of the 'lost city' of Atlantis may be used as a paradigm for Scottish invisibility in the early 20th-century — in fact, the myth of the lost civilisation, which vanished at its zenith, without a trace, and almost erased from collective memory except for a few elusive and fragmentary records, surfaces, in different shapes, in the works of a few Scottish writers in this period. Beside Arthur Conan Doyle's *The Maracot Deep and Other Stories* (1929), inspired by Professor Maracot's fictional discovery of Atlantis descendants in an underground refuge in the ocean, Lewis Spence — one of the most interesting representatives of the early Scottish Renaissance, who also, incidentally, met the disfavour of Hugh MacDiarmid — devoted four studies to the mystery of Atlantis (and others to ancient and vanished civilisations of Central and Southern America). The myth of the lost city is revisited imaginatively in his *The Plumes of Time* (1926), where Edinburgh is transfigured into an evanescent "Dunedin", suspended out of time and space, redolent with the aura of classical legends:

> She lies, this city of the air,
> Betwixt my hope and my despair,
> As the Nymphidian turrets lay,
> Close, yet a million leagues away.
>
> Her wynds' enchanted caverns hold
> Legend's invisible, fine gold,
> An hour sends greater glamour here
> Than Troy in twice a thousand year. [4]

The misty immateriality of Edinburgh (a "Naples of the sky"[5]) turns it, in "The Prows o' Reekie", into an enchanted ship, which sails across the Mediterranean, as if in search of its lost self and, juxtaposed with its ancient coastal cities, triumphs by comparison:

> O wad this braw hie heapit toun
> Sail aff like an enchanted ship,
> Drift owre the warld's seas up and doun
> And kiss wi' Venice lip to lip,
> Or anchor into Naples Bay
> A misty island far astray,
> Or set her rock to Athens' wa',
> Pillar to pillar, stane to stane,
> The cruikit spell o' her backbane,
> Yon shadow-mile o' spire and vane,
> Wad ding them a'! Wad ding them a'! [6]

That the myth of Atlantis — which at the turn of the century haunts the imagination of many European and American writers and readers — did take on a distinctive significance in Scotland is perhaps more evident in the work of James Leslie Mitchell ('Lewis Grassic Gibbon'). Readers will remember his *Three Go Back* (1932), a Wellsian romance, where the survivors of an air-crash discover that they have travelled back in time some 25,000 years to reach the lost continent of Atlantis — a pre-historical land where hunters roam free from the ties and restrictions of civilisation. Mitchell stresses the continuity between the present and this utopian world by having his protagonists rescue the hunters from the threat of the war-mongering Neanderthalers and escort them safely to the fertile eastern regions of the continent and "into the beginnings of history"[7]. The novel enacts a re-appropriation of the history of Atlantis, as it becomes clear in the words of one of the protagonists, who decide to take action and change this remote past in order to redeem their future: "How if the history we knew is the history we helped to build?"[7] The redemption lies not only in the discovery of a lost and forgotten civilisation, but in making it 'real' and relevant in the protagonists' present:

> She knelt beside him. "I'm going to do what you are going to do. Go back to the world we came from. Tell them we survived the *Magellan* — and then preach Atlantis till our dying day!"[9]

Even more significant, because classified as a scholarly and historical work, is Mitchell's lengthy *The Conquest of the Maya* (1934). The author, described by his publisher, Jarrolds of London, as "one of the leading authorities on American archaeology", in fact, was neither an archaeologist nor a trained historian, even though he went to the extent of reading some three hundred books on the topic in the British Library and succeeded in persuading quite a few scholars that he had indeed "explored extensively among the Maya remains in Central America".[10] While the book reveals — exactly like *Three Go Back* — Mitchell's fascination with the anthropological theories of Diffusionism, which denounced the loss of freedom and happiness brought about by civilisation (in tune with other anti-evolutionary theories of the period), it also intersects with the author's interest in 'lost' histories. In a letter to his former headmaster at Arbuthnott school, Alexander Gray, he had revealed his ideas on the origins of the Maya: "For I'm quite convinced that the Maya civilization was not indigenous to Central America but originated in Atlantis — or at least in Antillia".[11] Beyond any consideration of the theories espoused by Mitchell, it is interesting to see that the inquiry into the 'mystery' of the origins as well as of the rapid decline of this ancient civilisation has a remarkable relevance in his study, surfacing also in his scholarly essays on the subject. In "The end of the Maya Old Empire"[12] (1930), for example, he surveys the different hypotheses about the abrupt end of the Mayas, as well as the distorted report of their 'primitive' state spread by Cortes' historians in the Old World. Mitchell's is not exactly an anti-colonialist statement (readers who are familiar with Tzvetan Todorov's indictment of the violent subjection of the Maya by the Spanish conquerors in his *The Conquest of America* will certainly be disappointed), rather, as a diffusionist, he believes that the Maya and the Spanish civilisations, being both at an advanced stage, were equally barbarous and cruel. Mitchell, as an 'archaeologist', is more fascinated and concerned with the possibility of restoring some form of relative 'truth' to the lost and mistold story of the South American civilisation. In his introduction to *The Conquest of the Maya* he hints at this possibility, suggesting a relativism which is somewhat reminiscent of Sir Walter Scott:

> Witnesses are mistaken, scripts prevaricate, and mendacity is the child of excavation. . . . Nevertheless, deal in fantasy though he may, the historian's task is still plain: to attempt with good will and care the disentanglement of contemporary desire or distaste from the face of antique times. . .[13]

That *The Conquest of the Maya* is dedicated to Alexander Gray, makes the connection between Mitchell's native Mearns and the Yucatan peninsula somewhat more tangible. In this respect, the famous "Note", prefacing *Sunset Song* (1932), one of his best-loved novels, also rings like an archaeologist's manifesto, committing the author to the rescue of his native language (Scots) from literary oblivion. Most Scottish readers will remember the poignant words with which 'Lewis Grassic Gibbon' announces his original experimentation with his native tongue:

> If the great Dutch language disappeared from literary usage and a Dutchman wrote in German a story of the Lekside peasants, one may hazard he would ask and receive a certain latitude and forbearance in his usage of German. . . . The courtesy that the hypothetical Dutchman might receive from German a Scot may invoke from the great English tongue.

As in Mitchell's *Three Go Back*, Gibbon's reclaiming of Scots is a two-way journey: back to the past, to unearth what time has hidden from our sight, forward to the present, to make the re-discovered heritage a live tool again — as if "the history we knew is the history we helped to build". There is, of course, a strong line of continuity connecting this 'militant' re-reading of the myth of Atlantis with the interest of post-Union writers in disappearing/disappeared phases of civilisation, from James Macpherson to Sir Walter Scott, even though the somewhat passive 'line of resistance' offered by previous generations has now turned — at least in Gibbon — into a progressive project of reform.

If Lowland Scottish culture and language underwent a partial eclipse in the period following the Union, for the Highlands the eclipse was total, as pointed out before, Gaels ended up representing indeed a class of 'outsiders within'. From the harsh legal measures which followed the second Jacobite rebellion and which aimed at erasing their culture and language, to more recent forms of exclusion or marginalisation — suffice it to mention Trevor Roper's description of this culture as non-native ('Irish' rather than 'British')[14] which evidently points towards a lesser form of citizenship — Gaelic Scotland has remained, well into the 20th century, utterly isolated and secluded, as Aonghas MacNeacail has effectively evoked: ". . .there are hidden islands of us in the cities, holding on to who we think we are, or trying to create ourselves anew" [15]. Much 20th-century Gaelic literature can be described as a counter-narrative, that is a conscious effort to re-write what official history had distorted or obliterated. MacNeacail's "oideachadh ceart/a proper schooling" is dedicated to two writers, one Caribbean, the other African — respectively John Agard and Jack Mapanje — with whom, as a Gael, he shares the traumatic experience of diaspora and a similarly deeply-rooted mistrust of 'history':

nuair a bha mi òg	when I was young
cha b' eachdraidh ach cuimhne	it wasn't history but memory
. . .	
cha b' eachdraidh ach cuimhne	it wasn't history but memory
long nan daoine	the emigrant ships
seòladh a-mach	sailing out
tro cheathach sgeòil	through a fog of stories
mu éiginn morair	of landlords' anguish
mu chruaidh-chàs morair	of landlords' distress
mun cùram dhan tuathan,	their concern for their tenants,
mu shaidhbhreas a' feitheamh	the riches waiting
ceann thall na slighe,	beyond the voyage,
long nan daoine	the emigrant ships
seòladh a-mach,	sailing out
sgioba de chnuimheagan acrach	a crew of starved maggots
paisgte na clàir,	wrapped in their timbers,
cha b' eachdraidh ach fathann	it wasn't history but rumour [16]
. . .	

'Invisibility' in Scotland pertains to other natives — women being undoubtedly the most conspicuous group, at least in numerical terms. Silenced or marginalised as authors well into the 20th century, represented in literary texts according to a male gaze, when they speak with their own voice they unsettle, consciously or unwittingly, established ideas on gender and/or national identity. "As a woman I have no country. As a woman I want no country. As a woman my country is the whole world"[17], Virginia Woolf had declared in *Three Guineas* (1938), thus launching her critique of the nation as an expression of bellicose colonial masculinity. It would be difficult to contradict her, insofar as the modern nation, born out of the industrial revolution, shaped itself on a strict class and gender division and specialisation of roles. Her lesson had an enormous impact on successive generations of feminists, who questioned nationalism as an expression patriarchal ideology, on the grounds that "no nationalism in the world has ever granted women and men the same privileged access to the resources of the nation-state".[18] Scottish cultural nationalism — as Christopher Whyte has pointed out in his ground-breaking study — has been no exception, founding its definition on a canon of prevalently male authors and of literary texts centred on iconic male figures, from MacDiarmid's 'drunk man', to Gunn's overpowering male protagonists and MacIlvanney's ideal of 'heroic masculinity'.[19] There is no doubt that — in post -Union Scottish literature — some of the most impressive challenges to current constructions of gender and nationhood are to be found in women's writing. Susan Ferrier, for example, in her *Marriage* (1818) subtly challenges what could be described as a pillar institution of Victorian society, as well as a focal expression of discrimination against women, insofar as married women — it should be remembered — lost all their civil rights. The novel is remarkable — as we have partly seen — not least because it is populated almost exclusively by female characters, portrayed in their multi-faceted social, regional and individual varieties (thus effectively counteracting current stereotypical representations), while men remain quite marginal in the narrative, and certainly never seem to be up to the privileged role that society assigns to them. It is through her main character, the virtuous (almost perfect) Mary Douglas, daughter of an English mother and a Scottish father, raised and educated in Scotland by an enlightened adoptive mother, that Ferrier manages to convey her most innovative ideas. Crucial, in this respect, is her conception of education (Ferrier's key concern in this novel) — which, in the author's vision, should aim at supporting gently rather than directing and manipulating a young person. Education, therefore, can never replace experience and personal observation:

> Mrs. Douglas had sought to repress, rather than excite, her sanguine expectations; but vainly is the experience of others employed in moderating the enthusiasm of a glowing heart — Experience cannot be imparted: We may render the youthful mind prematurely cautious, or meanly suspicious; but the experience of a pure and enlightened mind is the result of observation, matured by time.[20]

It is from this firm conviction that much of Ferrier's ideology stems : if an individual's identity is the outcome of experience rather than inheritance or imposition of external ideas, then even family bonds and nationhood are the outcome of complex individual and social negotiations rather than 'fixed' factors, dependent on blood relations. Mary Douglas (who is the daughter of an exceptionally bad biological mother and is rescued and raised by a caring and affectionate adoptive one), like other characters in the novel, is an in-between — in many ways loyal to her native Scotland, she is however also aware of the complex intersections linking England to Scotland, and herself to both countries. Through her eyes we perceive the instability and artificiality of both gender and national constructions, as conveyed by one of the English (male) characters:

> 'Young ladies are much more housewifely in Scotland than they are in this country,' continued the Doctor ... 'at least they were when I knew Scotland . . . I studied physic in Edinburgh, and went upon a tower through the Highlands. I was very much pleased with what I saw, I assure you. Fine country in some respects — nature has been very liberal.'[21]

Here, Scotland is conceived as the land of 'nature' and, conversely, we infer, England stands for 'civilisation', correspondingly, women in Scotland are 'housewifely' and in England they are 'fashionable'. Mary Douglas does not object to the Doctor's clichés in words — she contradicts them, unwittingly, with her complex experience and superior wisdom. Susan Ferrier, in her novel, articulates a proudly Scottish stance — she resorts to Scots in her dialogues, she portrays her native country with obvious affection — and yet goes a long way to promote an idea of national identity which is, in many ways, remarkably ahead of its times.

Yet another woman, Nancy Brisson Morrison, in *The Gowk Storm* (1933) — like the previous novel a female *Bildungsroman* — questions, albeit in an indirect way, the exclusion of certain individuals/groups from representations of Scottishness. Narrated in the first person by the youngest of three sisters and set in the Highlands, it tells the doomed love story of the eldest girl and the dominie — a Gael who has recently moved to the village, and who is soon discovered to be a Catholic. Morrison stresses the 'otherness' of Mr MacDonald from the very beginning:

> The dominie came forward to greet us. His broad shoulders wore a deprecating stoop, as though apologising for his height, and he spoke in the slow, concentrated English of a Gaelic speaker. His low voice had a curious effect on his listeners. It was like a voice heard in lonely, echoing places; his words seemed to linger in the air long after he had spoken, as a twig still trembles when the bird has flown.
>
> There was something almost foreign in his appearance . . . [22]

An initial feeling of suspicion soon gives way to stern disapproval ("Whit we feel regret aboot, Mr MacDonald . . . is that ye didna tak' us into your confidence to the extent o' telling us ye were a Roman Catholic" [23]), and to outright ostracism, when the village gossip superstitiously marks him as an evil presence, endowed with demonic powers:

> 'When Homish MacLeod fell frae the Dingwall's loft . . . his leg bent under him and he fell on top o' it. The dominie cam' running to him, and pu'd at his leg and crackit it and held it in his twa hands. . . . Homish was running aboot next day wi' no e'en a hirple. [24]

Doomed to isolation, he is eventually forced to leave the village. The language of the novel is subtle and minimalist — there is no space for high-pitched expressions of hatred or passion. "He was dead to us after that spring" [25] is the narrator's laconic way of disposing of the dominie. Her voice is always ambiguously suspended between adherence to the villagers' views and disapproval of them, as in the short episode which relates a much quicker and crueller response on the part of the small Scottish community to a group of 'intruders'. 'They' (quotation marks stress peremptorily the distance separating them from the villagers) are gypsies, temporarily camping in a small clearing:

> 'They' were burying Hester's boy, they told us and their dark eyes watched us fearfully as though the properties of life and death lay in our hands. He had died last night. 'They' had asked several of the crofters' wives to come and see him to tell them what was the matter with him, but none of them would come. We were not surprised, for well we knew the fear with which the crofters and farmers regarded those dusky aliens who kept to themselves with the aloofness of royalty.[26]

Patriarchal rule (represented by the girls' rigid and authoritarian father, and by the elders of the village) is exposed with a similar ambiguous poise — human affairs in this beautifully written novel seem to be utterly governed by fate, and individual passions and projects appear to be doomed from the very beginning. And yet, the very choice of representing — thus of making visible — these 'exiles' in their own country is, in the context of the 1930s Scottish novel, in itself radical.

In much more recent times, a Glasgow born writer and artist of Scottish and Ghanaian descent, Maud Sulter, has confronted subtler forms of exclusion than those tackled by Ferrier or Morrison. "Close your eyes and imagine a German", is the refrain of her prose-poem "Blood Money"[27], telling the story of Monique, a Cameroonian girl who moves to France in 1926 and during the German occupation is sent to die in a concentration camp, wearing an inverted black triangle — Sulter (who has appropriated Alice Walker's famous quotation — "As a black person and a woman, I don't read history for facts, I read it for clues"[28]), is committed to retrieving the erased history of blacks because "if you do not recognise the constant black presence in Germany since the 15th century then you owe them no debt"[29]. An apparently 'innocent' act, like imagining nationhood becomes the starting point and the justification for all successive exclusions and persecutions — erasure from a country's history is a symbolic gesture that leads, or may lead to, genocide. Sulter — who regards her Scottish roots as very influential in her upbringing as an "image maker in words and pictures", especially as far the Glasgow oral and theatrical traditions are concerned[30] — does not refer explicitly to her native Scotland, yet she implicitly alludes to the 'invisibility' of Scots of an African descent or origin over the centuries.

In a different way, even though with equal commitment, Jackie Kay, a poet and a novelist of Nigerian descent, often refers to her experience as a black adopted child in a prevalently white Glasgow, where she is never considered (fully) Scottish:

> walking by the waters
> down where an honest river
> shakes hands with the sea,
> a woman passed round me
> in a slow watchful circle,
> as if I were a superstition;
>
> or the worst dregs of her imagination,
> so when she finally spoke
> her words spliced into bars
> of an old wheel. A segment of air.
> *Where do you come from?*
> "Here," I said, "Here. These parts."[31]

And yet Kay, brought up in Glasgow by white adoptive parents, is linked to her home town by a special bond of affection, and manifests an even more deeply-felt Scottishness than Sulter, both in her poems and in her fiction.

Most Scots will probably share with many Europeans today the impression that blacks are a recent ethnic presence in their country

— surveys of their history in Scotland are in fact very recent and scanty, dating mainly from the 1990s onwards, the first substantial study being represented by the National Library of Scotland's 1982 exhibition on "Africa and Scotland". June Evans, in her study *African/Caribbeans in Scotland* (1996),[32] provides a valuable investigation of this field, as well as a critique of a "'common-sense' view unchallenged until recently, that Scotland has 'good relations because there is no racism here'"[33], demonstrating that while "British racism is as much Scottish as it is English, Welsh and Irish"[34], intolerance to ethnic minorities has remained 'invisible' for a longer time north of the Tweed. Certainly not many Scottish readers are aware, for example, that the oldest extant racist literary text in Britain is a satiric poem by William Dunbar, "Ane Blak Moir", where the Makar described jokingly the African 'lady of tournament' at the court of James IV, the "ladye with the mekle lippis", as an "aep" ('ape')

> Quhou schou is tute mowitt lyk an aep,
> And lyk a gangarall onto graep,
> And quhou hir schort catt nois up skippis,
> And quhou schou schynes lyk ony saep,
> My lady with the mekle lippis.[35]

According to recent studies, the poem also testifies to the presence of black ladies and gentlemen, who moved freely about the country and were respected guests of the Scottish King. The lady in question obviously had a central role in both banquet and tournament, and there is evidence of other Africans attending the court of James IV.[36] Racism and ostracism against coloured people did not appear and root in Scotland until after the Union of 1707, when Scots became heavily involved in the slave trade and started investing extensively in the West Indies plantations. Black servants then became fashionable in Scotland, as in England, and they would often be included in family portraits, only to be covered by paint at a later stage, when slavery was outlawed in Britain and the presence of a black boy standing by the well-to-do would have been cause for embarrassment, and no longer a sign of social distinction. A few of these paintings, sent for conservation and x-rayed in recent years, have revealed the painted out black figures. "The Glassford Family" (c. 1767), by Archibald McLauchlin, held at the People's Palace in Glasgow, thus becomes an a eloquent symbol for the invisibility of 'second class' citizens in Britain. Much of Maud Sulter's visual art revolves around this theme, for example when she challenges the conventions of western art by 'imposing' on European stereotypical settings the cut-out and collaged figures of African icons and portraits in her series "Duval et Dumas" (1993), or by deploying herself as a model to represent the lost image of Jeanne Duval (the 'black' muse of Baudelaire) in her sequence of photographs "Les Bijoux I-IX" (2002).

A challenging exploration of the theme of 'invisibility' is offered by *Joseph Knight* (2003), an intriguing historical novel by James Robertson, constructed around the mysterious story of a concealed figure in a Scottish 18th-century painting — the portrait of the Wedderburn brothers in Glen Isla (Jamaica), at the sugar cane plantation named after the Scottish village where the eldest, an exiled Jacobite rebel, had sought and found shelter after the defeat at Culloden in 1746. The painted out image turns out to be that of their servant-slave, Joseph Knight, whose true story the novel re-tells, with detailed historical accuracy: Joseph, who had been compelled to leave Jamaica with his master and settle as his house servant in Scotland, appealed to the Edinburgh Court, and won his freedom, on the grounds that slavery, still legal in Jamaica, had already been outlawed in Great Britain. The 1778 Knight vs. Wedderburn case was unprecedented in Britain and became a leading one. Robertson's work is remarkable in its challenging revision of one of the most dramatic and contradictory chapters in Scottish history. Crucial events like the Jacobite rebellion and its aftermath and the revolts of the slaves in Jamaica against their Scottish masters (most of whom were Jacobite exiles) are for the first time treated side-by-side in a Scottish novel and their interconnectedness is thus exposed. The novel is also remarkable in its reconstruction of the complex debate pro- and anti-slavery: the strength of the Scottish economic interests in the Jamaican plantations and the blatant hypocrisy of those who did not tolerate slavery in their own country and yet thrived on the wealth produced by slaves in the West Indies are highlighted in the third part of the novel ("Enlightenment") through the voices of illustrious characters (such as Johnson and Boswell, Maclaurin and Hailes) as well as of commoners. While voices overlap and contradict each other — the climax is represented by the trial, which brings to the forefront, in a verbal duel, the two opposing factions — Joseph Knight, as a character, remains significantly 'silent' for most of the narrative. An object of hate, curiosity, or concern, he becomes a subject only at the end of the novel, when he speaks for himself, for the first time, and points out how his legal victory was, in fact, not 'his' at all. The juxtaposition between the 'freedom' of the ex-slave and that of the ex-Jacobite rebel (John Wedderburn), fully re-admitted to Britain's social and political life, is undoubtedly striking:

> 'I am calm,' he said. 'I have learned since that day what it is to be free. It is not to be free at all. I am well used to it now, so I am quite calm about it.'
> . . .
> 'I was made a slave before I knew what freedom was, and when they gave me my freedom they left me stuck here. I could not go back to Jamaica. I could not go back to Africa. I could not go home. They had left me no such place. . . . John Wedderburn, he came home. When I think of the grievous wrong he did me and all those other people on his plantations, it makes me angry even now that he, who was a rebel against his country, should be welcomed back. . . . But for me, once they had used me as a symbol for their justice, they did not care about me as a man.' [37]

Any free man and woman in Scotland is invisible, his Scottish interlocutor replies. Knight knows this not to be true: "Invisibility is not freedom if you are black. I'll tell you what it is to be black and invisible in this country: it is the proof that they choose not to see us."[38]

References

1   Edward Said, *Orientalism*, Harmondsworth: Penguin, 1991, p.21.

2   Ibid.

3   Alan Riach, "Introduction", in *Hugh MacDiarmid, Contemporary Scottish Studies*, Manchester: Carcanet 1995, p.viii.

4   Lewis Spence, "Dunedin", in Lewis Spence, *The Plumes of Time*, London: George Allen and Unwin, 1926, p.35.

5   Ibid.

6   Lewis Spence, "The Prows o' Reekie", in Lewis Spence, *The Plumes of Time*, London: George Allen and Unwin, 1926, p.54.

7   James Leslie Mitchell, *Three Go Back*, Edinburgh: Polygon, 1995, p.190.

8   Ibid., p176.

9   Ibid., p.194.

10   Obituary in *Welwyn Times*, 14th February 1935.

11   Letter to Alexander Gray (13th June 1929), National Library of Scotland, Acc.26019.

12   James Leslie Mitchell, "The End of the Maya Old Empire", in *Antiquity. A Quarterly Review of Archaeology*, Vol.IV, No.14, 1930, pp.285-302.

13   James Leslie Mitchell, *The Conquest of the Maya*, London: Jarrolds, 1934, pp.18-19.

14   Hugh Trevor-Roper, "The Invention of Tradition: The Highland Tradition of Scotland", in Eric Hobsbawm, Terence Ranger (eds.), *The Invention of Tradition*, Cambridge: Cambridge University Press, 1992, pp.15-16.

15   Aonghas MacNeacail, "I'm on a Train Again", in Aonghas MacNeacail, *Rock and Water*, Polygon, Edinburgh, 1990, p.103.

16   Aonghas MacNeacail, "oideachadh ceart/ a proper schooling", in *A Proper Schooling and other poems/ Oideachadh Ceart agus dàin eile*, Polygon, Edinburgh, 1996, p.13.

17   Virginia Woolf, *Three Guineas*, London: The Hogarth Press, 1938, p.197.

18   Andrew Parker, Mary Russo, Doris Summer, Patricia Yaeger (eds.), *Nationalisms and Sexualities*, London: Routledge, 1992, p.6.

19   Christopher Whyte, "Introduction", in Christopher Whyte (ed.), *Gendering the Nation: Studies in Modern Scottish Literature*, Edinburgh: Edinburgh University Press, 1995, pp.x-xi.

20   Susan Ferrier, *Marriage*, Oxford: Oxford University Press, 1997, p.222.

21   Ibid., p.235.

22   Nancy Brisson Morrison, *The Gowk Storm*, Edinburgh: Canongate, 1989, p.26.

23   Ibid., p.76.

24   Ibid., p.83.

25   Ibid., p.94.

26   Ibid., pp.35-36.

27   Maud Sulter, "Blood Money", in Lubaina Himid (ed.), *Syrcas*, Wrexham: Library Arts Centre, 1994, p.31.

28   Mark Haworth-Booth, "Maud Sulter. An Interview", in *History of Photography*, Vol.16, No.3, 1992, p.265.

29   Ibid.

30   Ibid., p.263.

31   Jackie Kay, "In my country", in *Other Lovers*, Newcastle upon Tyne: Bloodaxe Books, 1993, p.24.

32   June Evans, *African/Caribbeans in Scotland. A Socio-Geographical Study*, 1996, PhD Edinburgh University.

33   Ibid., p.83.

34   Ibid.

35   William Dunbar, "Ane Blak Moir", in *The Poems of William Dunbar*, J. Kinsley (ed.), Clarendon: Oxford University Press, 1979, p.106.

36   See Mary E. Robbins, "Black Africans at the Court of James IV", in *Review of Scottish Culture* Vol.12, 1999-2000, pp.35-45.

37   James Robertson, *Joseph Kinght*, London: Fourth Estate, 2003, pp.325-326.

38   Ibid., p.326.

EIGHT

'Polychromata' : towards a prismatic view of identity.

Many-coloured? It is one of the names of our little Cairo — Polychromata. She has many names, the Gift of the River, and nowhere do her colours flaunt as here, in the Khalig el Masri. . . . Key-colour to the kaleidoscope, master-note in the syncopation — it is Quest.

James Leslie Mitchell ("Polychromata I: He Who Seeks", 1929)

There is, in fact, a curious protean quality about Grieve's work; he can change into many characters, and is just as capable of writing bad poetry as of writing good. Sometimes these characters take on new names — noms de guerre rather than noms de plume . . . The situation occasionally allows two or more turns of the screw, as when the disguised poet not only calls himself something else, but actually turns out to be someone else . . . This is a phenomenon for which we need to invent a designation, I'd like to suggest 'Alias MacAlias' . . .

Hamish Henderson (Review of *The Uncanny Scot* by H. MacDiarmid, 1969)

'Protean' writers, who either use one or more literary pseudonyms, or who cast conflicting self-projections (or 'masks') onto the 'stage' of their works, abound in the history of post-Union literature. James Macpherson, for example, reached both fame and notoriety as 'Ossian', while his life was spent between Badenoch and London — a revered Bard in his native country and a member of the British establishment and of the House of Commons in the capital city of the Empire. Robert Burns's work has only recently been reappraised for the formidable heterogeneity of the *personae* staged in his poems, and the analogous variety of styles, registers and modes that they display. Sir Walter Scott became famous as 'The Author of

Waverley' — editors, antiquarians, historians assumed the many roles played by Scott-writer, in a disquieting game of mirrors that continually defers the truth and puzzles the reader. James Hogg ('the Ettrick Shepherd'), like Burns, wrote in a number of different 'voices' and styles — the romantic novelist, the Scottish ballad-writer, the outspoken and well-read 'rustic' ('The Shepherd') who contributed to the *Blackwood's* "Noctes Ambrosianae". His contemporary John Wilson — poet, novelist, editor, Professor of Moral Philosophy at the University of Edinburgh — also contributed to the popular series of the "Noctes Ambrosianae" as 'Christopher North'. The use of pen-names, which is certainly not an uncommon practice in 19th-century Scottish literature, intensifies remarkably, almost alarmingly, in the early 20th century: the Scottish reader will surely be familiar with a series of well-known 'double names', such as William Sharp/ 'Fiona MacLeod', Edwin Muir/ 'Edward Moore', James Leslie Mitchell/ 'Lewis Grassic Gibbon', Helen Nora Wilson Low/ 'Lorna Moon', Christopher Murray Grieve/ 'Hugh MacDiarmid' (to mention just his best known pseudonym), Thomas Douglas Macdonald/ 'Fionn MacColla'. In fact, a thorough survey of the literary history of this period, will yield the names of many more similarly 'janus-faced' writers, most of whom have been, by now, consigned to oblivion. Finally, as far as Scottish Gaelic writers are concerned, a 'double name' cannot be but the norm — Sorley Maclean is best known in Britain by his English name, but his Anglophone readers are likely to be familiar also with the Gaelic one (Somhairle MacGill-Eain), as both appear, side by side, in the bilingual editions of his poems. 'Doubleness', in this case, can be described as an institutionalised practice (diffused by histories and anthologies of Scottish literature) and it points towards an 'external', and ostensibly more 'objective' cultural and linguistic split than the above-mentioned cases. However, there is no doubt it is no less a source and a reflection of a problematic/problematised identity, as we shall see in the present chapter.

The pen-name/alter ego phenomenon was so extensive by the mid-20th century that it could not fail to catch the attention of

readers and critics outside Scotland. The captivating definition of
this 'syndrome' — 'Alias MacAlias' — is in fact borrowed by Hamish
Henderson from an article which appeared in *The New Statesman* in
the mid-1960s,[1] according to which Scottish writers have a "well-
known penchant . . . for operating under cover of pseudonyms . . .
[and] . . . a surprising number have chosen and still choose a new
moniker, and by the same token an alter ego."[2] Henderson's article
is interesting not simply insofar as it records and labels this trend,
but also because it provides a cultural and ideological explanation
to its diffusion in Scotland — a 'defence', almost, against those who
might find this an eccentric and even improper practice, or an
attempt to escape from one's 'true' identity:

> Owing to the constant fruitful interaction of folk-song and art literature
> in our tradition, we're often faced with the sort of set-up in which no
> one can say for sure where MacAlias ends and Anon begins. A sort of
> friendly communal cannibalisation has therefore been the rule rather
> than the exception in Scottish literature. . . . [3]

Henderson, here, is writing specifically about Hugh
MacDiarmid's work and his occasional appropriation of other
writers' words, to which he "gave poetic shape — thus affording
them a new and more permanent habitation, and a name"[4].
However, even though his analysis is persuasive, if slightly biased
towards a re-definition of Scottish literature as characterised — in
compliance with the Renaissance ideological orientation — by a
'democratic' inclination, it can only partly account for a
phenomenon which is too extended and much more complex than
his approach can possibly cover.

This idea of a distinctive Scottish (literary) 'split personality'
syndrome is not new in itself, and it finds its most striking
counterpart on a thematic level — readers from all over the world
are certainly familiar with the many and famous Scottish stories of
duality and divided selves. In Scott's *Redgauntlet* two narrators
complement and mirror each other, and also act, as characters, as
the two sides of the same person; in James Hogg's *The Private Memoirs*

and Confessions of a Justified Sinner the theme of the double self finds
its roots in the Calvinist obsession with the conflict between eternal
opposites; *Marriage*, by Susan Ferrier, explores the opposite fates of
two twins, separated soon after their birth, and raised by different
mothers in different countries (Scotland and England); in
Stevenson's works — *Dr Jekyll and Mr Hyde* has become the 'archetype'
narrative of this genre — the same obsession extends to embrace
the vaster province of morality and of a society (the Victorian one)
which is divided against itself. The theme of the double is, in fact, a
recurring one in European and American 19th-century fiction (Mary
Shelley's *Frankenstein*, Melville's *Moby Dick*, Oscar Wilde's *The Picture
of Dorian Gray* are just a few eminent examples) — it would be
imprudent to circumscribe it as uniquely Scottish. Yet, from the
above-mentioned examples, it is obvious that this theme does have
a local twist and a special relevance in Scotland. In Scott and Ferrier,
for example, the divide seems to run along (and to question) the
English/Scottish identity boundary. Even the London setting of *Dr
Jekyll and Mr Hyde* mirrors the split 'spaces' of the Old Town and the
New Town in the author's native Edinburgh, where two worlds
run in parallel, connected and separated by distinct and yet partly
overlapping architectural plans. On one side the well-lit,
symmetrical and rational burghs of the Enlightenment, on the other
side the uneven, irregular, dark and 'unreasonable' medieval tangle
of steep and narrow alleys.

The 'duality' running through Scottish literature has been
described and accounted for in different ways at different times,
until it gradually established itself, in the first half of the 20th
century, as one of the main distinguishing features of the Scottish
tradition. Gregory Smith, in his *Scottish Literature: Character and
Influence* (1919), introduced the idea of a 'Caledonian antisyzygy',
that is of a continuous tension and fluctuation between opposite
tendencies, a love for 'domestic' realism on one side and a love for
the supernatural and the fantastic on the other. MacDiarmid
followed in Gregory Smith's footsteps in this articulation of the
"polar twins of the Scottish Muse" — a descriptive model he found

useful to counteract Victorian stereotypes of the Scot as a canny and parsimonious peasant. In a period when talking about a 'national psyche' was regarded as an acceptable practice, Muir also referred to the 'antisyzygy' — in his controversial *Scott and Scotland* — as a distinctive trait of a tradition that was doomed to extinction. If MacDiarmid inhabited proudly and blissfully the place "whaur extremes meet", Muir thought (with T.S. Eliot) that this tension only prevented his country producing an organic culture and prophesied its demise. James Leslie Mitchell/Lewis Grassic Gibbon, as we shall see, performed the divide in his country's culture by staging two distinct *personae*, the first (Mitchell) coinciding with the English writer, the second with his Scottish counterpart — besides having distinct attitudes and interests, each of his 'literary selves' would use his own personal typewriter, and each would pose differently for official photographs. Mitchell was the one in profile, Gibbon would face the camera and had a pipe in his mouth. [5] The success of Gregory Smith's thesis and term (embraced with enthusiasm by Kurt Wittig in his *The Scottish Tradition in Literature*, 1958) testifies both to the need, in this period, to provide distinctive 'labels' for Scottishness, and also to the fact that it does really capture something crucial about post-Union Scottish literature and culture. If England has managed to construct itself as an organic, cohesive culture, Scotland (which defines itself, by necessity, against England, and against England's perception of Scottishness) gradually constructs its 20th-century identity by revaluating that very duality (or plurality) which had been regarded as a sign of cultural weakness. An article which appeared in the *TLS* in 1938 articulates effectively the typical prejudice of the centre against the Scottish 'polyphonic' tradition — the author's use of clichés hardly needs comment in this context. Significantly, while the plurality of voices and styles of "a country so thinly peopled and so remote from the rest of Europe" is considered remarkable there is no doubt that it also reveals "some sense of deficiency":

> Most Scots who care at all about writing must have felt, from time to time, that the phrase 'dying of a hundred good symptoms', which Pope used of himself, had a certain application to their national literature. .

> . . . Set down in order, the varied characteristics of Highlander and
> Lowlander display powers which we all know to be singularly
> noticeable in Scottish writing: a love of words and phrase-making
> inherent in the race, fanciful imagination, a sense of colour, a sense of
> rhythm . . ., a masterly use of the weird and the grotesque, sardonic
> humour and a keenly critical — sometimes too critical — eye for the
> human comedy. . . . . There is that peculiarly Celtic passion for home
> and land, a worship of place which has nothing to do with worship of
> nature and the good brown earth, but rejoices in topography as in some
> force bolstering up the ego of the writer. There is the poetry of exile,
> the poetry of death and grave; there are ribald satires and glorious
> ballads and exquisite songs . . . .[6]

Variety and heterogeneity may be attractive, but at the end of
the day they are perceived as a sign of cultural inferiority.

If Scotland defines itself, in the course of the 20th century,
against the rooted myths of cultural cohesion and national unity,
then it is not surprising that the most poignant discussion and
representation of a Scottish 'un-organic' or 'divided' identity has
been articulated by a Gael. The cultural and linguistic split affecting
Gaelic Scotland is, in fact, deeper and more tangible — almost
'physical' — than in the writers above mentioned. Iain Crichton
Smith's tormented and surrealist 'double man' —Murdo Macrae —
narrator and main character of three narrative sequences, both
embodies and glosses such a split. Murdo, who grows up on Harris,
is lucidly and painfully aware of his being caught in-between two
worlds and two languages. It is this very consciousness that makes
him a total misfit, an isolated character, doomed to a self-reflexive
life, who experiences a daily short circuit in communication. His
self-conscious 'doubleness' turns him into the 'jester', the medieval
'holy fool' of the village — the one who 'sees', and for this he is
laughed at and scorned:

> . . . One half of Murdo, vertically visualised, had the colour red: the
> other half had the colour black. Also it seemed to him that half his
> tongue spoke Gaelic, the other half English. There was a smell of salt
> herring from the black half, and a smell of bacon from the other half.

He also at first wrote Gaelic with his right hand and English with his
left hand. Later these physical processes were reversed. In periods of
stress he was completely immobilised, i.e. he could not write at all. . . .
When he was at home the colour black pulsed, and when he was in
school the colour red glowed. [7]

If Murdo is a 'double man', haunted by his red-black vision, so
is Smith, who has appointed him as his alter ego (*Thoughts of Murdo*,
1993) and has used him as a voice to tell the story of his life (*The Life
of Murdo*, 2001) in what can be described as a 'deferred'
autobiography ("Using 'Murdo' rather than 'I' allowed me the
distance that I needed to be objective about myself and to make
comedy of painful experience."[8]). Smith has also discussed at length
the predicament of what he describes as the "linguistic double
man"[9], that is of a bilingual "riddled with guilt"[10] (by 'turning his
shoulders' to his native Gaelic he feels he is betraying it) and
haunted by a sense of inadequacy ("I write in English which is
probably, in some ways, unknown to me, a Highland English"[11]).
With Wittgenstein, Smith believes that we are shaped by the
language that we speak, and not viceversa — in this perspective a
bilingual becomes a sort of 'freak', doomed, as Murdo is, to the
impossibility of communication, caught, as he is, in the gap that
separates the two codes. The gap paralysing him is, however, —
quite obviously — not merely linguistic, but also historical and
cultural, between a 'majority' culture and a 'minority' one,
hegemonically related and which have constructed themselves, in
the course of time, in a similarly monolithic fashion, against which
Murdo's hybridity is bitterly resented. It is once more in a poignant
autobiographical note that Smith articulates his painful plight of
in-betweenness — in terms that are certainly familiar to many a
post-colonial writer — with a touch of his characteristic, surrealist
brand of humour:

I am, I suppose, indeed the double man, a kind of monster, an Incredible
Hulk that slouches somewhere to be born. But where is that
somewhere? I doubt very much it is Bethlehem. It may be in a No Man's

Land between the two languages. It may be where no one has been before. It may lie somewhere between Lewis and Wittgenstein. [12]

In more recent times, the self-deprecatory attitude which has dominated the debate on constructions of Scottishness in the past century has given way to a full appreciation of a 'mongrel' and 'syncretic' culture, key terms in the descriptive model of Scottish culture adopted, for example, by Angus Calder[13], and of a literary tradition which has a "special affinity for polyphonic texts" where, "as it is no longer possible to speak of a centrally unified nation, so, too, the unified subject of individual identity has come under question", as phrased by Roderick Watson.[14] While syncreticity and polyphony are not unique to Scottish culture and literature (as they mark, in different degrees, all cultures and literatures), it is true that Scotland, like other countries, has been led (almost compelled) by historical contingencies to represent its identity in layers. In this context, the empathic reappraisal of the Scottish tradition and the sense of identification with it expressed by one of the most famous Caribbean writers, Wilson Harris, indeed throws a 'bridge' between two cultures which were incidentally inter-connected by a coloniser-colonised relation in the course of the 18th and the 19th century:

> The Scottish element was, curiously, an implicit strand, ringing a bell of recognition for me. There was something in Kurt Wittig [*The Scottish Tradition in Literature*, 1958] I recognised at once ... When I read Wittig's description of the strange subjectivity of the Scottish imagination I felt as if I was at home.[15]

Countries like Scotland and the Caribbean, culturally and linguistically layered — Harris contends — are bound to be charged by a high creative potential (a 'Creative Schizophrenia'), which is fully accomplished by those writers who are aware of this complexity and are able to "bring all the layers into play".[16] Harris, who speaks from the vantage point of an extra-European culture, and therefore of a culture that has always consciously defined itself against the centre in terms of polyphony/polycentricity, is certainly more extreme than his contemporary Scottish colleagues in his emphasis of these same terms as descriptive of Scotland's culture:

> ... There's the Europe we know now and underneath that there is the Europe of the Renaissance and underneath that again there is the Europe of the Middle Ages. There is the Europe in which Mary Queen of Scots and John Knox were contemporaries. There are these different Europes. And Scotland in a way may be a microcosm of them all ... You have a whole theatre in Scotland ...[17]

Harris' vision of Scotland as a polyphonic, syncretic 'theatre' is of course a joyous one, and contrasts with at least a century of guilt-ridden writing on the 'failure' of Scottish culture and nationalism on the part of Scots, and of denigration from the centre. It is, however, crucial to stress that not all contributions by Scottish intellectuals were characterised by a negative attitude. There are exceptions, represented by some 20th-century writers' challenging appropriation and redeployment of the categories of identity themselves (national, ethnic, gender-based), which points towards a drastic revision of the very idea of identity as a 'prismatic', rather than a monolithic configuration[18]. One of the writers who best represents this positive trend is James Leslie Mitchell/ 'Lewis Grassic Gibbon' — the idea of a 'prismatic' identity has been, in fact, borrowed from his fiction. The epigraph to his first novel, *Stained Radiance* (1930), is from Shelley's *Adonais* ("Life, like a dome of many-coloured glass,/ Stains the white radiance of Eternity", ll. 462-3), and presents us with an image which is recurrent in his work. Mitchell's prism is suggestive of a vision of movement, fluidity and of interconnectedness among the colours of the spectrum, as opposed to the immobility and fixedness of eternal (platonic) forms. The image had already been used by Mitchell in *Polychromata*, a short story cycle published in *The Cornhill* between 1929 and 1930. The sequence was successively re-published — with a few alterations — in one volume as *The Calends of Cairo* (1931). The title of the original sequence, however, is more telling of Mitchell's ideological stance than that eventually agreed on with Jarrolds, clearly chosen as a more marketable and attractive one, and as more appropriate (if less imaginative) for a series of 'exotic' tales set in the Middle East. Mitchell's *Polychromata* stories can hardly be regarded as aesthetically outstanding or formally innovative — on the whole they can be said to conform largely to the tenets of 'colonial' literature. However, there are a series of features which point towards a different approach than that displayed by most 'Oriental' tales written in this period. There is, for example, sheer delight in the polymorphous and polyphonic texture of the colonial society of the Middle East, where he was stationed as a simple soldier with the British Army, between 1919 and 1923:

> If you sit long enough in the Khalig all Cairo will sometime pass by — boyar and beggar, brown man and black, and the men of the shades of white, and all the women of the history of the world, the vile and the fair and the pitiful. And you will hear the drifts of all speech and all passion, all hope and all desire if you sit and listen in the Street of All Egypt, that is older in soul than the Ramesids and so young that it rides the electric-tram. [19]

Interestingly, Mitchell, unlike most of his contemporary fellow countrymen, does not seem to fear miscegenation. Quite a few of his characters, in *Polychromata*, are 'racially mixed', most are ethnical hybrids or live on the borderline of two or more cultures and languages — as the narrator/protagonist Anton Saloney, the Russian déraciné, "dragoman, guide, ex-colonel of horse in the army of Deniken, and one-time Professor of English Literature in the *Gymnazium of Kazan*"[20], who tells his story in English because "only this wayward, featureless, fatherless tongue may sing our *Polis Polychrois*"[21]. Mitchell does not succeed in eluding entirely contemporary racial stereotypes — in fact he stumbles over quite a few of them, even in his second 'Oriental' story-cycle *Persian Dawns, Egyptian Nights* (1932). And yet his 'polychromatic' perspective, his focussing on fluidity and permanent change, and on corporeal, contingent reality is a first step towards that re-definition of identity that post-colonial and gender studies have articulated in very recent times, and according to which:

> Cultural identity . . . is a matter of 'becoming' as well as of 'being'. It belongs to the future as much as to the past. It is not something which already exists, transcending place, time, history and culture. Cultural identities come from somewhere, have histories. But, like everything which is historical, they undergo constant transformation. . . . identities are the names we give to the different ways we are positioned by, and position ourselves within, the narratives of the past.[22]

"I am rooted but I flow"[23] Mitchell could have said, with Virginia Woolf — readers who are familiar with his Chris, the famous heroine of *A Scots Quair*, are likely to have a good idea of a representation of identity as 'becoming'. Chris is ever changing, flowing, 'thinking through her body', as when — quite often in the course of the trilogy — she looks at herself in the mirror, or in a pool of still water, and records change in corporeal terms:

> She bent over there through the rushes . . . and looked down at her face in the water. It rippled a moment, it was brown with detritus, at first she could see nothing of herself but a tremulous amorphousness in the shade of the rushes; and then the water cleared, she saw the flush below her cheek-bone, her own face strange to her this last month and stranger now. [24]

For Chris "nothing endures" — she appropriates the Heraclitean motto to describe the mutability of human things, the impossibility of grasping and fixing them. There is often, in her words, a sense of loss:

> . . . she saw the trail of the mist, great sailing shapes of it, going south on the wind into Forfar, . . . past Brechin smoking against its hill, with its ancient tower that the Pictish folk had reared, out of the Mearns, sailing and passing, sailing and passing, she minded Greek words of forgotten lessons, *Παντα ρει. Nothing endures.*[26]

A similar representation of identity as 'becoming', equally conscious, and definitely more positive, is that of Hugh MacDiarmid

who, in *A Drunk Man* (1926), used the metamorphic Thistle image
as a transformative account of (Scottish) identity. In the poem the
Thistle conveys all the multifarious and contradictory questions
the Drunk Man explores. The Thistle is seen as "a mongrel o fire
and clay", a "skeleton at a tea-meetin' ", it is compared to the sound
of bagpipes, it is a sea of "green tides", and a "barren twig", it is like
Moses's "burning bush", until all its contrary qualities are brought
together in the "Ygdrasil", the tree of life in Scandinavian mythology.
Hybridisation and pastiche techniques, along with 'plagiarisms',
provide a formal and linguistic counterpart to the image of the
'prismatic' Thistle — satire, ballad, philosophical dissertation,
parody are but some of the genres that intermingle to give life to a
stunning modernist poem, which also displays a Joycean polyglot
delight in the interplay of Scots diachronic and synchronic varieties,
English, and a number of other languages. 'Mongrelism' (what we
would call today 'hybridity'), celebrated creatively in *A Drunk Man*,
is theorised with lucidity by MacDiarmid in several of his articles
and essays, as a crucial interpretative model of Scottish culture:

> From the Renaissance point of view, on the contrary, it is claimed that
> it is utterly wrong to make the term 'Scottish' synonymous with any
> fixed literary forms or to attempt to confine it to any particular creed
> or set of ideas — let alone to such notions as are really part and parcel
> of Scottish degeneration and provincialism.[26]

A less known and yet enticing 'polychromatic' Scottish writer
is the *emigré*, Lorna Moon (neé, Nora Wilson Low 1886-1930), who,
born in Strichen, in North-Eastern Scotland, established herself as
a freelance writer in the USA (she is perhaps best known in her
native country for her story cycle *Doorways in Drumorty*, 1925, which
represents a delightful subversion of the Kailyard novel) as well as
one of the most famous screenplay writers for silent films in
Hollywood between 1921 and 1930 — her collaboration with Cecil
B. DeMille and with Frances Marion certainly contributed
considerably to her fame in this field. Lorna Moon was also a
formidable fabricator of 'fictions of herself' — she left behind her so

many conflicting versions of her life, that it has become almost impossible to disentagle 'fact' from 'imagination' ("she told so many false stories about herself" her third and most famous child as well as biographer — Richard DeMille — laments [27]). Moon was not so interested in constructing a coherent alternative *alter ego* rather, the principle that presided over her diverse and contradictory accounts was based on the necessity or inspiration of the moment. She claimed that she was a descendant of Highland chiefs, or that she had been kidnapped and had been compelled to marry as a young girl, that she was a widow of war, or a divorceé, that she had grown up in a Scottish 14th-century mansion and that she had blue blood in her veins — none of these details were in the least truthful. Even her photographs belie a similar 'kaleidoscopic' restlessness — the image changes she undergoes are quite striking for the historical period in which she lived. In some pictures we see her posing sensuously, lying on a couch, with a huge 'Catholic' crucifix looming behind her (even though she was an atheist with a Presbyterian background); in another series of portraits she appears as an innocent, romantic heroine, her dreamy face framed in auburn curls; in yet another sequence she stands out as an aggressive and *à la page* modern woman, exhibiting a black bob and fresh nose surgery. The contradictory representations of herself — literary or visual — that she fabricated (drawing liberally from current clichés) point towards an idea of identity that is 'performative' — that is, an identity without an 'essence', with no ontological status apart from the various acts which constitute its reality, as contemporary 'queer theorists'[28] today would explain. The comparison with the contemporary media icon Madonna may seem anachronistic, yet it is not entirely out of place — by impersonating/parodying different and contrasting cliché identities, Lorna Moon ends up challenging their 'essence', thus relativising their absolute truth, as it were, and asserting that it is what you *do* at particular times, rather than a universal who you *are*, that, in the end, matters.

In more recent times, Scottish literature has contributed towards a re-definition of the idea of individual identity as a continuum, a flexible and open status, through the work of a series of challenging women writers. A.L. Kennedy, for example, questions bitterly standard assumptions of both national and gender identity by articulating a position of in-betweenness, or of downright unease with traditional definitions. In *So I Am Glad* (1995) she presents us with an emotionally damaged character — Jennifer — who feels painfully displaced, within her family, her country and even within herself:

> I didn't understand my father or my mother. I didn't understand my country, its past, its present, its future, its means of government or the sense of its national anthem and flag. When I was young I didn't understand the other children and the adults were just as bad. Then I became an adult and nothing had changed. I didn't understand Steven, or anyone else of my intimate acquaintance, up to and of course including me. I never really understand me.[29]

A.L. Kennedy's heroines (like Helen in *Original Bliss*, 1997) are often estranged from their world, abject, dangerously and precariously hovering on a borderline — they resist being 'overdefined' as 'women', both from a patriarchal and a feminist perspective. As Ali Smith has aptly observed: "her female characters are always individuals before they are women"[30]. Furthermore, like many Scottish contemporary literary characters, even Kennedy's heroines resent an 'overdefinition' of Scottishness, which had tyrannised previous generations:

> As far as I can understand, my entire country spent generations immersed in more and more passionate versions of its own past, balancing its preoccupations with less and less organised activity or even interest in the here and now.[31]

"By sharing my intimate, individual humanity", A.L. Kennedy explains, "I hope to communicate a truth beyond poisonous nationalism or bigotry"[32] — *beyond* is, in fact, a keyword in her writing, which promotes an idea of identity only partly and loosely anchored to the traditional categories of 'gender' and 'nation'.

Kate Atkinson (a Scottish based author), in her *Behind the Scenes at the Museum* (1995) — set in her native Yorkshire — similarly introduces a woman protagonist/narrator who relates her voyage in search of her (feminine) identity.[33] Hers is also a voyage in the past, as she collects the fragmentary memories of the story of her mother and her female lineage across two centuries of Yorkshire history, and weaves them into her present — her native county, in this sense, is a 'museum of memories', inhabited by the ghosts of its past. Ruby Lennox tells her story like a contemporary Tristram Shandy, in what develops as a refined, parodic, metafictional mode of narration. The opening page of the novel is telling in this respect — announcing a non-linear progression (the intertextual relation to Sterne's masterpiece is plain) as well as the impossibility of clearly separating 'fact' from 'fiction':

> I exist! I am conceived to the chimes of midnight on the clock on the mantlepiece in the room across the hall. The clock once belonged to my great-grandmother (a woman called Alice) and its tired chime counts me into the world. . . .

> We live in a place called "Above the Shop" . . . The Shop . . . is in one of the ancient streets that cower beneath the looming dominance of York Minster. In this street lived the first printers and the stained-glass craftsmen . . . Guy Fawkes was born here . . . and Robinson Crusoe, that other great hero, is also a native son of this city. Who is to say which of these is real and which a fiction? [34]

In this way the self-conscious narrator introduces herself, starting her dialogue with the reader: the present of her narration is juxtaposed, in the text, with the past, fragmentarily recorded in a complex system of 'footnotes'. Ruby's narration creates, through memory, a matrilinear pattern, a sense of belonging to a women's 'collectivity' that presides over the shaping of a harmonious relation between past and present, private and public, histories and History, across the fragmentariness which characterises both the formal structure of the text and the narrator's experience.

Jackie Kay also uses memory (and music) as a harmonising principle over the multi-layered, fluid configuration of the main character's identity in *Trumpet* (1998) — Joss Moody. Joss, a renowned jazz trumpeter, Scottish by mother, African by father, woman by birth, man through choice, seems the perfect embodiment of that idea of identity as not connected to an 'essence', but instead free-floating and anchored only to performance, articulated by queer theorists. Joss's life is reconstructed through the non linear, non chronological sequence of the memories evoked by his wife, his adoptive son, his friends and acquaintances when, after his death, the shocking truth about his biological identity is revealed. The witnesses' voices mingle and overlap in the novel, weaving Joss's multiplicity into an intense and compelling portrait, but also talking about themselves, the fragmentariness and displacement of their existences. Music (jazz) and memory are indissolubly linked at the very beginning of the novel, in the epigraph, a quotation from George Gershwin: "The way you wear your hat;/ the way you sip your tea,/ The memory of all that —/ No, no! They can't take that away from me." At the close of the novel the cohesive power of music becomes clear, as Joss, playing his trumpet, is able to create a new unity out of the fragments of his life:

> ... he is the whole century galloping to its close. The wide moors. The big mouth. Scotland. Africa. Slavery. Freedom. He is a girl. A man. Everything, nothing. He is sickness, health. The sun. The moon. Black, white. Nothing weighs him down. Not the past or the future. . . . He just keeps blowing. He is blowing his story. His story is blowing in the wind. He lets it rip. He tears himself apart. He explodes. Then he brings himself back. Slowly, slowly, piecing himself together.[35]

Kay — a Scotswoman of Nigerian descent and an adopted child — has often centred her poems on the issue of ethnic/national/ gender identity, as in her poem "Pride", revolving around an imaginary encounter on a train (in an ideal suspension from time and space) with her African self (the "black man" who soon after leaves her alone with her reflection on the "dark train window"). Here, the poet stresses the dynamic, open configuration of identity, by staging an ideal dialogue, an active exchange between the speaker's 'selves':

When I looked up, the black man was there,
staring into my face,
as if he had always been there,
as he and I went a long way back.
He looked into the dark pool of my eyes
as the train slid out of Euston.
For a long time this went on
the stranger and I looking at each other,
a look that was like something being given
from one to the other. [36]

Is it then possible — in the light of the issues and authors analysed so far — to discern a distinctively Scottish contribution to the re-definition of identity? Perhaps it is: post-Union Scottish literature does indeed represent a journey through unsettled and unsettling identities, as claimed before in the present volume. The problematisation of national identity has, inevitably, encouraged the questioning of wider identity issues, in a process of relativisation of established truths that has characterised many colonised cultures. As Salman Rushdie has pointed out, from a dislocated subject's perspective reality is never 'what it is', rather it is perceived as a transient, artificial construction. Rushdie refers to migrants in particular, but, as we have seen, the experience of dislocation can be cultural as well as physical:

> [...] the triple disruption of reality teaches migrants: that reality is an artefact, that it does not exist until it is made, and that, like any other artefact, it can be made well or badly, and that it can also, of course, be unmade. [37]

The notion of identity undergoes a similar disruptive process, as in (post-)colonial societies many factors contribute towards the unsettling of its traditional construction — we could easily replace the word 'reality' with 'identity' in the above quotation, and obtain an equally effective description of a similar process. In this context, it is worth remembering that Scotland not only shares with such societies this particular experience, but, as it boasts one of the longest, or possibly, "the longest continuing example of a substantial body of literature produced by a culture pressurised by the threat of English cultural domination"[38], it is not out of place to claim that many of the themes and issues developed by many post-colonial cultures in the course of the 19th and 20th century were already present in Scottish literature in the 18th century.

It is equally important — by way of conclusion — to stress that Scottish culture has produced (and preserved) traditions or myths which oppose the constructions of reality and identity promoted by European middle-class, capitalist societies. One such myth is appropriated by Christopher Whyte in *The Warlock of Strathearn* (1997), a novel set in 17th-century Scotland, at the time of the persecution of witches. A subtle web of intertextual references (Scott and Hogg being the most conspicuous ones) firmly links this text to the Scottish tradition of romance and historical novel, while the Warlock, around whose story the novel revolves, takes us to a pagan world of magic metamorphoses (opposed, in the novel, to the monotheistic severity of the Presbyterian church). A wizard of multiple becomings, he often describes with relish the freedom and the exhilaration as well as the voluptuousness of giving up the human form:

> I had been a kingfisher, a gnat, and an owl, to mention only a few of the transformations my physical part had been subject to, and my body had a provisory feel to it even during the years when it never shifted from the human.[39]

The Scottish Warlock, who pushes his transformation skills to the extreme by becoming a woman (described as the most exacting of all his magical enterprises), thus poses the ultimate challenge to the idea of morphological normativity at the heart of western civilization — anthropocentric and grounded, as Rosi Braidotti observes, on "Leonardo's figure of the naked, male, white body, which allegedly constitutes the measure of all things"[40] — by asserting the value of other (even non-human) 'embodiments'. Commenting on the severe condemnation of his magic metamorphoses by the fundamentalist Minister he observes ". . . I cannot believe that whoever, or whatever created this world would be angered to see its repertory of living creatures extended"[41]; when he turns himself into a woman he wonders: "In changing sex, had I become normal at last? What did normality mean?"[42]

Thus the Warlock is not simply the anachronistic champion of a 21st-century philosophy of 'becoming', rather than 'being' — he also makes us see that that philosophy of becoming — although long sidelined and persecuted — is a strain of Scottish/European culture. The point is not to know who you are — the Warlock tells us — but what, at last, you want to become: "It is belief that shapes reality".[43]

References

1   Hamish Henderson, [Review of] *The Uncanny Scot: A Selection of Prose* by Hugh MacDiarmid (*Scottish International*, 1969), in Hamish Henderson, *Alias MacAlias. Writings on Songs, Folk and Literature*, (Alec Finlay ed.), Edinburgh: Polygon, 1992, p.305.

2   Ibid.

3   Ibid.

4   Ibid.

5   Interview with Ray Mitchell, in *Welwyn Times and Hatfield Advertiser*, 19th March 1976.

6   Doris N. Dalglish, "Towards a Nationalist Literature. The Scottish Renaissance", in *Times Literary Supplement (Special Section. 'Scottish Literature Today')*, 30th April 1938, p.x.

7   Iain Crichton Smith, *Thoughts of Murdo*, Nairn: Balnain, 1993, pp.11-12.

8   Epigraph in Iain Crichton Smith, *The Life of Murdo*, Edinburgh: Birlinn, 2001.

9   Iain Crichton Smith, "The Double Man", in R.P. Draper (ed.), *The Literature of Region and Nation*, London: Macmillan, 1989, p.137.

10   Ibid., p.140.

11   Ibid., p.139.

12   Ibid., p.145.

13   Angus Calder, "A descriptive model of Scottish culture", in *Scotlands*, 2.1, 1995, pp.1-14.

14   Roderick Watson, "Postcolonial Subjects? Language, Narrative Authority and Class in Contemporary Scottish Culture", in *The European English Messenger*, Vol.2/II, 1998, pp.21-31.

15   "Wilson Harris Interviewed by Alan Riach", in Wilson Harris, *The Radical Imagination: Lectures and Talks*, Alan Riach and Mark Williams (eds.), Liége: L3. Liége Lang & Lit, 1992, p.63.

16   Wilson Harris, "Unfinished Genesis: A Personal View of Cross-Cultural Tradition", in ibid, p.102

17   "Wilson Harris Interviewed by Alan Riach", in ibid., p.64

18   For the choice of the 'prism' as a metaphor for identity I am partly indebted to Giovanni Covi's critical work on Jamaica Kincaid. See Giovanni Covi, *Jamaica Kincaid's Prismatic Subjects. Making Sense of Being in the World*, London: Mango Publishing, 2003.

19   James Leslie Mitchell, "Polychromata II: The Epic", in *The Cornhill*, Vol.LXVII, August 1929, p.162.

20   James Leslie Mitchell, "Polychromata I: He Who Seeks", in *The Cornhill*, Vol.LXVII, 1929, p.7.

21   James Leslie Mitchell, "Polychromata II: The Epic", in *The Cornhill*, Vol.LXVII, August 1929, p.160.

22 Stuart Hall, "Cultural Identity and Diaspora", in Patrick Williams and Laura Chrisman (eds.), *Colonial Discourse and Post-colonial Theory; a Reader*, Hemel Hempstead: Harvester Wheatsheaf, 1993, p.394.

23 Virginia Woolf, *The Waves*, London: Grafton Books, 1977, p.69

24 Lewis Grassic Gibbon, *Sunset Song*, in *A Scots Quair*, London: Pan Books, pp.105-106.

25 Ibid., pp.117-118.

26 A. McIntyre (ed.), *Hugh MacDiarmid: Contemporary Scottish Studies*, Edinburgh: Scottish Educational Journal, 1976, p.83.

27 Richard de Mille, *My Secret Mother, Lorna Moon*, New York: Farrar, Strauss and Giroux, 1998, p.259.

28 Queer theorists in the past decade or so, have examined the way in which individuals perform their identities and the cultural values that write the 'scripts' of their 'performances'. See Judith Butler, *Gender Trouble: Feminism and the Subversion of Identity*, London: Routledge, 1990.

29 A.L. Kennedy, *So I Am Glad*, London: Vintage, 1996, p.p.65-66.

30 Ali Smith, ""Four Success Stories", in *Chapman*, 74-75, 1993, p.181.

31 Ibid., 187.

32 A.L. Kennedy, "Not Changing the World", in Ian Bell (ed.), *Peripheral Visions: Images of Nationhood in Contemporary Fiction*, Cardiff: University of Wales Press, 1995, p.102.

33 See Gaie De Zambiesi, Kate Atkinson, ovvero la memoria di lei: trecce di un viaggio alle scoperta di sé, (Tesi di Laureo, Université di Trento, 2001).

34 Kate Atkinson, *Behind the Scenes at the Museum*, London: Doubleday, 1995, pp.9-10.

35   Jackie Kay, *Trumpet*, London: Picador, 1998, p.136.

36   In Kevin MacNeil, Alec Finlay (eds.), *Wish I Was Here. A Scottish Multicultural Anthology*, Edinburgh: pocketbooks, 2000, p.160.

37   Salman Rushdie, "Günter Grass", in Salman Rushdie, *Imaginary Homelands*, London: Granta, 1991, p.280.

38   Robert Crawford, *Devolving English Literature*, Oxford: Oxford University Press, p.8.

39   Christopher Whyte, *The Warlock of Strathearn*, London: Victor Gollancz, 1997, p.113.

40   Rosi Braidotti, *Metamorphoses. Towards a Materialist Theory of Becoming*, Cambridge: Polity Press, 2002, p.123.

41   Christopher Whyte, *The Warlock of Strathearn*, London: Victor Gollancz, 1997, p.77.

42   Ibid., p.154.

43   Ibid., 208.

NINE

Dreaming Caledonia: Will there be a Scottish literature?

Memory is the seamstress, and a capricious one at that. Memory runs her needle in and out, up and down, hither and thither. We know not what comes next or follows after.

Virginia Woolf (*Orlando*, 1928)

…traditions are live and not passive things stuck in a closet but they are… made by human beings… they are recollections, they are customary practices, collective memory, they are all kinds of things, but they are certainly not the simple pure thing to which people return and get comfort in.…I firmly believe that it is a tremendous mistake to give up to tradition as much as is being given up to it…

Edward Said (Interview, 1997)

Is there an appropriate way to conclude this short excursion through such a vast and complex subject? Perhaps it is to address once more, T.S. Eliot's belligerent question ("Was there a Scottish literature?"[1]), and set it, provocatively, in the future: *will there be* a Scottish literature? Impossible as it is to forecast what will happen in this, as in any other field of human activity, the hope or fear for a better or worse tomorrow is undoubtedly what informs much of our present — an attempt to reply (with all due caution) to this question is, therefore, also a way of 'making sense' of our journey through several centuries of Scottish literary history.

One, first conjectural reply to the title question could be — '*Too much*'. One of the risks that an observer of today's Scottish cultural scene may envisage is, in fact, that of its 'overdefinition', which would represent indeed the death of the protean, polyphonic tradition described in the pages of the present volume. Such a step might be encouraged (somewhat paradoxically) by the fact that the formalisation of a 'canon' of Scottish literature is now — for the first time — required with the demand for the creation of a 'national' school curriculum and, more generally, as a consequence of a growing international awareness of Scotland's cultural autonomy from England. If European established nation-states have become more 'laid back' about defining themselves, Scotland has not entirely shed the defensive urge to fix the contours of its cultural identity. The risk of 'overdefinition' has already turned into a near-reality with the recent establishment of Irvine Welsh's *Trainspotting* (1993), along with a host of other young, talented and equally 'acid' writers, as an international paradigm of Scottishness — the virulently anti-romantic myth promoted in their works has been incidentally further reinforced by the international success of the 2003 film version of Alexander Trocchi's *Young Adam* (1957), the archetypal 20th-century *écossais maudit*. The 'fault' — as it were — does not lie, quite obviously, with the subject of urban degradation and drug-culture or with the demotic style that are the special marks of this 'post-realistic' genre (which does indeed represent a challenging and distinctive strain in recent Scottish fiction) — but rather with the fact that, through a process of novel exoticisation, these particular themes and style today quite narrowly define Scottish literature in the eyes of the international reading public, with the complicity of the book industry, ever in search of marketable icons and labels. That new clichés — however topical or trendy — should replace the much criticised old ones is of course not a desirable exchange.

The challenge for the near future, then, is not to define Scottishness in more suitable or convenient terms, let alone to produce further totalising views of Scottish culture, but rather that of *dedefining* it, as Robert Crawford has phrased it recently [2], and of freeing it from the cage of those "pernicious discourses" into which it has been confined for the past two centuries — "Tartanry, Kailyardism, and Clydesideism"[3] — and which still largely inform representations/perceptions of Scotland, in literature as well as in film.

In fact, a call for 'de-Scotticising' Scottish literature has been on the agenda of many writers for quite a while. If some Scottish Renaissance representatives — as we have seen — warned against the risks of too narrow a definition of their culture, it is especially in the 1980s and even more so in the 1990s that writers begin to feel uneasy with what they perceive as a 'literary ghetto'. Iain Crichton Smith, for example, certainly went a long way to distance himself from any ready-made and crippling definition of Scottishness:

> Writing here in this room in Oban, what do I think of being, "a Scottish poet"? I don't think of being a Scottish poet at all, I think of the act of writing poetry. I know that more disabling choices are available for me here — shall I write in Gaelic or English? But at the moment of writing I do not think of these things. . . . When I have finished the poem I do not ask myself, "Is this a good Scottish poem?" I am aware of other poets, some Scottish, some not. . . . but in the end I ask myself, "Is this a good poem?" I do not ask whether my Scottishness will save it. I know that in the end it will be in some sense Scottish because it was written by me and I live in Scotland.[4]

In the first place — Smith reminds us, in his characteristically essential style — we have to ask ourselves not "why Scottish literature matters", but "why *literature* matters". Scottishness comes after — an unpredictable consequence of the literary text, and certainly not its active aim, even less its primary source of inspiration. Whatever it is that substantiates it, it can only be defined retrospectively.

That the myths of the nation, or rather their degenerations, however monstrous, are inescapable, has become a central postulate — significantly — in quite a few Scottish dystopic novels in recent years. Paul Johnston's 'Quintilian' crime fiction series (after the name of the investigator who is their hero and narrator) discloses before our eyes a very near future, so near that quite a few of the events narrated forebodingly overlap with our present. The first three novels (*Body Politic*, 1997; *The Bone Yard*, 1998; *Water of Death*, 1999), set in the 2020s, have as a backdrop Edinburgh, by now one of the independent city-states into which Britain has been fragmented following a catastrophic national and international crisis. The revolutionary movement which has led it to independence and to stability — 'the Enlightenment' — has drastically reformed its political and social organisation along the lines of Plato's *Republic*. Guardians rule, auxiliaries enforce the laws and citizens work like slaves in the tourism industry — the only source of income of the 'perfect city'. As in all literary visions of the future, the spotlight is very much on the present and its faults — Johnston's dark satire evidently addresses the vices of contemporary global society as well as some specific aspects of his native city and country. The future vision which unfolds before our eyes is all the more alarming as it mirrors, grotesquely, our present. Not too unrealistically, for example, Edinburgh has been degraded to a bleak 'touristland' — with visitors storming the Royal Mile all year round and revelling in what has become a 'permanent' Festival, with its generous offer of "cheap sex, horse-racing in Princes Street Gardens, casinoes . . ., whisky and tartan knitwear"[5]. Edinburgh readers are likely to have experienced a 'shock of recognition' when confronted with this fictional (but almost realistic) 'Disneyfication' of their culture. As national icons are ruthlessly commodified (the extreme example is possibly represented by a Mary Queen of Scots strip-teasing in one of the sex-joints which attract crowds of viewers in the ex-Old Town) we witness the degeneration and vilification of the (Scottish) nation and its myths. Significantly, if the empty symbols of Scotland's past nationhood are cannibalised, in a daily ritual, by hordes of non-sentient tourists, other, presumably more meaningful expressions of national identity are downright suppressed by the Guardians: "writing in any Scots dialect is right out"[6] for example ("I've forgotten all the dirty bits from Irvine Welsh books I memorised when I was a kid",[7] Quintilian remarks) and so is speaking in Scots, or even with an accent. Johnston's satire, however, becomes subtler when the 'myths of perfection' on which Scotland has constructed its distinctive national identity — the Enlightenment and the Church of Scotland — are clearly equated to Plato's totalitarian political ideals. That the revolutionary party calls itself 'Enlightenment' and shares with its 18th-century counterpart the same impulse towards the construction of a 'perfect city' or a 'city of reason' (to cover up and deny the 'unreason' of the original structure) is in itself an act of indictment — emphasised by Quintilian's perception that the Enlightenment conceals a "dark heart" beneath the geometrical linearity of its architecture ("I walked over to the edge that forms the centre of the circular street, and gazed into the darkness of the Enlightenment"[8]). The critique of the Enlightenment myth of the perfect city extends to include that of the Scottish Kirk (whose 'perfection' was sanctioned by the Solemn League and Covenant in 1643) — it is no mere chance, for example, that the Guardians in Johnston's dystopia have elected the Assembly Hall as their official meeting place:

> The Church of Scotland used to hold its annual gathering here. It was typical of the Council's desire to replace religion with its own philosophy that it chose this location rather than the former City Chambers or Parliament House. They probably had too many associations with democracy.[9]

That in Edinburgh, all citizens and auxiliaries are now compelled to attend weekly debating sessions on Plato's *Republic* provides an extra cross-reference to the Presbyterian practice of the Bible debating sessions, and so does the fact that the (atheist) Guardians of the Scottish Republic are often likened by Quintilian to fervent ministers ("The chief boyscout rose to his feet like a preacher about to address his congregation. . ."[10]) or downright Calvinist zealots.

If Johnston's satirical deconstruction of (national) myths of perfection is quite original, his overall vision is not too distant from that articulated by Alasdair Gray, for example, in *A History Maker* (1994) — where, in a 23rd-century globalised world, states still retain the 'banners' of a nationhood ritualised in not-so-harmless, even though carefully regulated and monitored, war games. The Global and Interplanetary Council for War Regulation, sitting in Geneva, has ushered humanity into a century of relative 'concord' — yet another rational Utopia — as Delilah the plotter explains to the world's great new war hero, the Scotsman Wat Dryhope:

> . . . the twentieth and twenty-first centuries played games that nearly destroyed everything animal but the cockroaches. Yes, a peaceful century of fighting-by-rule was needed to restore human resources. The eighteenth century was a bit like ours. European rulers feared the chaotic wars of an earlier age so their armies only fought at frontiers. Polite people toured each other's nations, visited each other's homes, whether their governments were warring or not. Those Europeans thought they were safer than the Imperial Romans, but boom! 1789! The French Revolution! A new age of warfare started which spread competing nations to every part of the globe.[11]

The dynamics of the nation-state, as represented in Gray's future vision, are inextricably intertwined with the dynamics of war — whether chaotic and wildly destructive, or contained and regulated, war is an essential part of the social life of a nation and faithfully reproduces the separation of public from private, of the particular from the universal, of the human from the divine, of the family from the state, and of the male from the female realms of experience and action underlying its construction. Warriors fight facing the 'public eye' (a moving camera which follows them in battle and televises their deeds all over the world), while women tend the hearth; men administer death in war, mothers honour the dead and procreate at home. Gray's post-modern novel plays with the western philosophical and political tradition, which separates, as theorised by Aristotle, the public realm of the *polis* (state, city, or republic), domain of the male subject, from the private realm, defined by the hearth and home as the *locus* of family and belonging to the wife/daughter/mother/sister — the former being the world of history, the latter a 'space' prior to or outside history. *A History Maker*, of course, goes a long way to deconstruct and destabilise the binary oppositions on which the nation is traditionally constructed, thus articulating a powerful and radical critique of all national myths.

Another intriguingly bleak vision of a future Scotland, this time the outcome of two centrifugal pulls — fragmentation and globalisation — is that depicted in Matthew Fitt's *But n Ben A-Go-Go* (2000), a SF-novel which is entirely written in a remarkably creative (and non-demotic) Scots. In an ironic reversal of the present world, Scotland, due to global flooding, is mostly underwater, with the exception of the Highlands (now called the 'Drylands') and of Port, a congregation of floating islands (or 'Parishes'), chained to the floor of the ocean and parched by a tropical sun. Among its inhabitants, the 'melanos' (dark-complexioned) represent the privileged class, as they can bear, unlike the 'albinos', the high temperatures and the fiery sun brought about by 'God's Flood' in 2039. In this context of reversed clichés, it is no surprise that the seediest quarter of Port should be 'Favela Copenhagen', inhabited by Danes and Norwegians "warsled wi aulder techonology"[12], who are presented as the dregs of society: "they were the maritime canton's scabby dugs, a raggle-baggle ermy o scaffies, dishcloots, cyberhoors an cludgie cleaners."[13] Parallel to this floating and unstable community, there is 'VINE' — cyberspace, an electronic universe, a virtual and infinite network of environments and situations into which characters delve and which they recklessly navigate. 'VINE' is the space of elating freedom, of infinite variety, of serious danger — very suggestively evoked by the narrator, who follows Paolo Broon, the protagonist, in his wild 'stravaigin':

> . . . Ayont he kent the infinite glen o cyberspace hotched wi randan variety. He had ayewis felt sae free stravaigin VINE, jouking fae yin hamesite tae the next, nebdivin intae its deepest neuks an acceleratin awa up tae zero air.
>
> A stushie o licht on the waw tae his left poued him oot o his dwam. A gowd oblong flichered a second then pixelled itsel thegither intae an auld-farrant letter-box. [...] A neat white letter strauchled oot. The page unfaulded itsel an Paolo, skellie-eed wi surprise, read the words: 'Bonnie Lemon's'. . . . [14]

Fitt's is a 'de-territorialised' Scotland, deprived of one its most powerful traditional national icons — the landscape — and already blending into the pluralised and globalised cyberscape of the postmodern age. The quickening domain of VINE erodes traditional divisions between the local, national and global, creating a new dynamic of re-arranged 'glocal' space, where it is the language of narration — a strikingly inventive Scots — that represents the only vestige of a nation conceived in territorial, cultural and ethnic terms.

A pull away from 'Scottishness', or rather from any direct involvement in (re)definitions of Scottishness, indeed characterises many young Scottish writers today, who seem to subscribe fully to what R.L. Stevenson said, far back in 1883: "Scotland is indefinable; it has no unity except upon the map"[15]. This idea of 'indefinability' goes hand in hand with the increasing loosening of the relationship between the national space and identity which has characterised the second half of the 20th century in many European countries — Scotland, in this respect, is no exception. Joy Hendry has explained this in plain and effective words: "there has been an increasing lack of need for us to talk about Scottish identity. . . . There is less need to talk about it, because we can be it, and, more importantly do it. Whatever it is."[16]

Will there be, then, a Scottish literature? A second, conjectural reply to the same question could be: 'Too many'. Linguistic regionalism and de-centralisation are strong trends in Scotland today — as in many parts of Europe. An archipelago of Scottish microcosms has been brought to (literary) life and is receiving attention from both critics and readers — Robert Alan Jamieson and Christine De Luca's Shetlandic poems may provide a useful example in this respect. The 'region' evoked by their respective collections (*Voes and Sounds*, 1994, by De Luca, and *Nort Atlantik Drift*, 1999, by Jamieson) is caught between its Norse past and its Scottish present, ever fluctuating between aloofness and integration with either time or culture, between public History and private stories, and finding its individual (and temporary) cohesion only in the literary space of the poems. This incessant movement of negotiation is visually evident in the tripartite structure of Jamieson's collection, where each poem in Shetlandic, usually revolving around a memory, personal or collective, of a fragment of landscape or of an event, appears side by side with an authorial gloss in English, which mediates between the 'here and now' of the reader and the geographical and cultural remoteness of the 'object', and by a translation in English. The single page thus represents iconically the gaps separating different voices — as different islands — in time and space, as well as the attempt at bridging them. There are silences which cannot be filled (as the tangible difference in language and lay-out of the Shetlandic poem and its translation imply) and yet some sort of communion can be achieved, as in "Sie-Færin", where the sea, predictably, offers a powerful metaphor of togetherness:

> Ayont da flat ært
> O da boondries o sens,
> He kens —
>
> Da wirld's choost
> A roond bloo baa fok sirkil
> t'wirk an liv.
>
> A gloabil awaarnis.
> Du spits ida oshin
> an a drap myght rekk Æshnis.
>
> Bit hoiest du a sæl
> du gjings quhar du will
> tæ njoo fun laand.
>
> *Beyond the flat earth of the boundaries of sense, he knows —*
> *The world is just a great round ball folk circle to work and live.*
> *A global awareness.*
> *If you spit in the ocean, that drop might reach the nearest shore.*
> *But hoist a sail, and you go where you please, to new found land.*[17]

If Jamieson speaks in three quite distinct voices, De Luca discards the devices of translation and authorial comment, and recurs instead to a discreet glossary to bridge the gap between

Shetlandic and English, the two languages which alternate freely in her collection. In this way, the two worlds and the two languages seem to coexist, side by side, and to blend one into another; however, the unfilled and unfillable gaps between them are still all there. We witness, for example, the same unresolved tension between a rural past ("Glancing backwards" is the title of the first sequence of poems in the Shetland dialect) and an urban present (as in "City Life", the first poem — in English — of the second sequence, entitled "Change"). Ultimately, De Luca's lyrical voice also modulates the three stances articulated in Jamieson's collection: that of the native Shetlander, that of the 'outsider', and that of the 'cultural mediator', who weaves lines of 'meaning' where they have been lost or never traced before — the outcome is a 'mobile' map of the Shetlands, a 'place' whose contours are continually renegotiated between the three different perspectives.

Irretrievable distance, in terms of space and time, for example, prevails in the air view of Orkney — the glance over the islands is unmistakably that of a stranger, who belongs to another time and another place:

> Outstretched below
> the isles of Orkney lie:
> skins of ancient monsters
> patterned wildly.
> Long sinuous members, golden fringed,
> sleep deeply, unstirring;
> great nostrils, quiet now
> lapping a tide.
> Abrupt headlands: lurking claws
> mindful of lost sea struggles.
>
> The sea, lightly creased,
> caressing her trophy,
> sings of the vanquished.[18]

The tension between the two worlds and their irreconcilable values, finds a tragic outlet in the last poem of the collection — significantly the only one written in English with facing translation in Shetlandic — evoking the oil tanker disaster which occurred at Quendale Bay in Shetland in January 1993. If Jamieson ends his collection with a celebration of 'togetherness', De Luca's sea, in the poem's last stanza, seals, protectively, the islands' seclusion and isolation:

The song of the sea	Da sang o da sea
Take no heed! Take no heed!	Never leet! Never leet!
I've danced and I've scolded	A'm danced an a'm flet,
drowned that stinking barrel.	Smored yon grötti-barrel.
I shall feed you: comfort you	I sal maet you;
with whitest surf.	cöllie aboot you
	wi whitest froad.[19]

At the beginning of the 21st century, attempts to construct a unitary, organic Scottish culture seem to have been left behind for good, as plurality has taken over: "I am very queasy about any attempt to integrate all the different Scotlands of history and the present into some bogus, essential Scottishness" Angus Calder has recently admitted, "nevertheless, I think I identify common continuities in the cultures occupying these expanses of territory..."[20] 'Regionalism' is a trend common to many European countries today — the term can in fact indicate projects of a very different ideological nature. If, for many, it stands for a closed and auto-referential devolution from the centre, and for an extreme protection against the 'dangers' of globalisation, for others it may indeed herald a "re-evaluation and critical redemption of space"[21] from now obsolete categories like the nation, and the emergence of other forms of individual and collective identity. Countries like Scotland and Ireland — as contended by Ray Ryan — can give a lead in this respect, as in both countries "regions were so culturally insulated that the concept of a national history is ... an invalid descriptive category"[22] — their literatures, significantly, go beyond the traditional idea of nation by reappropriating the regional and social spaces which compound it. Scottish and Irish literary texts thus represent, in Ryan's analysis, the flexible and sensitive cognitive maps of a fluid cultural territory which they themselves contribute to construct. In this way, from passive representations of 'real' geopolitical entities 'out there', or of traditional, predefined territorial objects, literary texts become one of the privileged sites of construction of new forms of (place-bound) identity.

It is undeniable that our conveniently conventional geopolitical imagination, which envisions and maps the world in terms of spatial blocs, territorial presence and fixed identities, is no longer adequate in a world where ontological purities are under eclipse, and it is equally indisputable that postmodernity is giving us a new geopolitics: in this context, countries like Scotland, which have been compelled to define themselves outside set conventions, are today providing a valuable alternative model to traditional categories. Is it then legitimate or advisable to try and trace lines of continuity in the complex archipelago of (post-national) 'Scottish' regional/social identities? What is it (if anything) that binds them together? In their introduction to *Being Scottish* (2002) — a series of personal reflections on Scottish identity by several interviewees from different backgrounds — Tom Devine and Paddy Logue isolate a common denominator among the manifold and dissimilar perspectives in "the importance of place, landscape and belonging"[23]. There is no doubt that 'place' (associated with memory and identity) and 'landscape' (in its ahistorical and purely 'geological' dimension) have been core components of Scottish identity in the past century — along with music, they are perhaps the most enduring icons of this country. Both Lewis Grassic Gibbon, in *Sunset Song* (1932), and Hugh MacDiarmid, in "On a Raised Beach" (1934), for example, refer to a land which is pre-historical or a-historical — 'geology' (respectively the red clay fields of the Mearns, or the grey stones of the Shetland) provides in both texts the 'core essence' around which the narrator or the lyrical voice constructs its sense of identity:

And then a queer thought came to her there in the drooked fields, that nothing endured at all, nothing but the land [...]. Sea and sky and the folk who wrote and fought and were learnéd, teaching and saying and praying, they lasted but as a breath, a mist of fog in the hills, but the land was forever, it moved and changed below you, but was forever, you were close to it and it to you, not at a bleak remove it held you and hurted you [...] [24]

I must get into this stone world now.
Rachel, striae, relationships of tesserae,
        Innumerable shades of grey,
        Innumerable shapes,
And beneath them all a stupendous unity,
Infinite movement visibly defending itself
Against all the assaults of weather and water,
. . . [25]

The poem "Hallaig" by Sorley MacLean/Somhairle MacGill-Eain is perhaps the most powerful expression of a 'sense of place' articulated in a 20th-century Scottish literary text. "Hallaig" is about time, memory and loss: it brings to life an 'emotional map' of the evicted village, but it also represents a sensuous (and joyous) celebration of the landscape. As Seamus Heaney has remarked, "MacLean's relation with his landscape is erotic... He has an epic poet's possession of ground, founders, heroes, battles, lovers, legends . . ."[26] — a 'possession' that is manifest already in the two opening stanzas:

Tha bùird is tàirnean air an uinneig
troimh 'm faca mi an Aird an Iar
's tha mo ghaol aig Allt Hallaig
'na craoibh bheithe, 's bha i riamh

eadar an t-Inbhir 's Poll a' Bhainne,
thall 's a bhos mu Bhaile-Chùirn:
tha i 'na beithe, 'na calltuinn,
'na caorunn dhìreach sheang ùir.
. . .

The window is nailed and boarded
through which I saw the West
and my love is at the Burn of Hallaig,
a birch tree, and she has always been

between Inver and Milk Hollow,
here and there about Baile-chuirn:
she is a birch, a hazel,
a straight, slender young rowan.[27]
. . .

An utterly different and more theoretically conscious approach
is that of Kenneth White, who, unlike MacLean, does not express
a sense of belonging to a place, but rather champions a generic
nomadic association with the land, beyond history, and beyond
any pre-ordained form of collective identity:

> . . . in France, if you come from Scotland . . . or anywhere else on the
> Celtic fringe, and scribble a page or two, you're a bard. . . . A bard is one
> who sings and re-sings the history of the tribe. Being without a tribe,
> and doing my damnedest to get out of history, I just can't be no beardy
> bard, OK?
>
> Call me Ishmael, intellectual nomad.
>
> I don't know whether I'm looking for a tribe. I don't think so (I
> prefer the company of secret and solitary minds like Scot Erigena and
> Duns Scot), but it's true I'm kind of interested in tribes right now.
> Maybe because I've had a bellyful of nations and states.[28]

White's vision owes certainly something to Gilles Deleuze and
Félix Guattari's theories of nomad thought and deterritorialisation,
only transposed, quite freely, on an imaginative level. His *The Blue
Road* (1983) is a book "of mental navigation, . . . crammed with
physical metaphysics and poetic cartography"[29], written in the form
of a travel notebook (which seems to anticipate Bruce Chatwin's
The Songlines, published in 1987), with personal annotations,
quotations, 'sketches' of the places visited, loosely connected
together by the protagonist's movement in space rather than by a
narrative thread. White's ambitious project is that of replacing the
traditional geopolitical vision with a 'geopoetical' one, aimed at re-
establishing a lost consonance between cosmos and conscience,
land and mind, nature and culture:

> Geopoetics goes with this all the way, convinced that the
> interconnection between the non-human and the human is very far
> from having been fully explored. Geopoetics is concerned with the
> development of that interconnection, and with its expression. . .[30]

To Alasdair Gray's *Why Scots Should Rule Scotland* (1997) goes the merit of articulating a more 'pragmatic' approach than White's 'theoretical' challenge of the traditional geopolitical vision. Betraying the expectations of those readers who might have been enticed by a vaguely 'Braveheartesque' title, he identifies the foundation for his Scottish(post)nation in geology:

> I argue that by being in Scotland you deserve a government as distinct from England as Portugal from Spain, Austria from Germany, Switzerland from the four nations surrounding her. My argument is not based on differences of race, religion or language but geology. Landscape is what defines the most lasting nations.[31]

This is no minor achievement: by implicitly severing the bond that traditionally links a nation (rigidly defined in terms of "race, religion and language") and its 'territory' (a term that stresses a relation of 'property' or 'possession'), Gray promotes an idea of 'nationhood' which finds its justification in the dynamic interconnection between the community and the 'landscape', which actively shapes the identity of the people, as much as the people, in the course of time, mark its contours. In the "firths, sea lochs, chains of high moorlands and mountains [which] made north Britain like a cluster of big islands jammed together in the east and coming apart in the west"[32] Gray, along with many Scottish writers of the 20th century, does not detect simply beauty. Their 'geopoetical' vision is perhaps best described by Édouard Glissant's words: "Describing the landscape is not enough. The individual, the community, the land are inextricable in the process of creating history. Landscape is a character in this process" . Glissant, born in Martinique, long recognised in the French and Francophone world as one of the greatest writers and thinkers of our times, turns the polyphonic and multi-layered reality of his native island into the complex, energetic vision of a world in transformation, and defines his "poetics of relation"[33]— both aesthetic and political — as a transformative mode of history. In Glissant's view, we come to see that 'relation' in all its senses — between wo/man and wo/man, between wo/men and their environment — is the key to transforming mentalities and reshaping societies. The highly innovative dimension of his vision and its evident intersections with similar stances articulated by Scottish writers demonstrate, once more, how marginality can indeed represent a source of unprecedented creativity, and also how, in order to articulate Scottishness, it is absolutely necessary today to look for comparative models. Scottish literature matters — this is beyond doubt — but it will have to be explained in other languages and to other cultures in order to survive. This, we feel, is the challenge for the new millennium.

What about our initial question: will there, after all, be a Scottish literature? As a scholar, of course, I cannot provide a reply to it. I can only try to chart and analyse, as honestly as possible, the past and the present — the future remains hopelessly beyond my scope. This does not mean that the future is not my concern, on the contrary: as a literary historian I unearth fragments of a past that has been erased or forgotten; as a teacher and a critic I have the task of making texts 'speak' to contemporary readers, thus making sure that they remain live for future generations; as the author of the present volume I hope that readers, within and without Scotland, will appreciate the immense interest of a complex, multi-layered tradition which has been neglected and marginalised for an incredibly long time. The future is a vital source of energy in our lives: we *have* to ask ourselves what it will be like, and yet it would be wrong and even dangerous to restrict it — this is, in a nutshell, the sense of the provocation behind the title of this chapter. So let us leave the question open for future generations. Let us leave them the freedom to tell who and what they are in their own words, by taking up and giving a new order and a new shape to the stories and the traces we will leave behind.

If, as a scholar I must refrain from replying to the questions I have provocatively asked, I may still be allowed to attempt an imaginative answer, as an appropriate way of concluding our literary journey. Let me try.

Scotland is a post-nation, a meta-nation, a geological nation: it is an imagi-*nation* and, as such, it is nourished by the aspirations and the dreams of its inhabitants. Dreams at times intersect and at times converge in some common ideal, be it William Wallace, a football team, Robert Burns or even, why not, as in David Greig's *Caledonia Dreaming* (1997), Sean Connery. Whether or not we achieve our dreams is not important, the very process of dreaming gives us something that shapes our present and moves us forward. MacDiarmid's words — originally referred to the protagonists of the Scottish Renaissance — convey exactly this idea and, with a slight adaptation, may provide an appropriately 'open' ending to this volume:

> Whether "dreamers of dreams" can still prove themselves "movers and shakers of the world" or not, the [writers of the Scottish nation] are dreaming the dream outlined in these pages. [34]

References

1   T.S. Eliot, "Was There a Scottish Literature?", in *Athenaeum*, No.4657, 1st August, 1919, p.680.

2   Robert Crawford, "Dedefining Scotland", in Susan Bassnett (ed.) *Studying British Cultures*, London: Routledge, 1997, p.96.

3   Douglas Bicket, "Fictional Scotland: A 'Realm of the Imagination' in Film Drama and Literature", in *Journal of Communication Inquiry*, Vol.23, No.1, 1999, pp.6-8.

4   Iain Crichton Smith, "A Poet in Scotland" (originally published in *The Scottish Review*, May 1982), in *Towards the Human. Selected Essays by Iain Crichton Smith*, Edinburgh: MacDonald Publishers, 1986, p.84.

5   Paul Johnston, *The Bone Yard*, London: Hodder and Stoughton, 1998, p.89.

6   Paul Johnston, *Body Politic*, London: Hodder and Stoughton, 1997, p.19.

7   Ibid.

8   Ibid., p.308.

9   Ibid., p.23.

10   Paul Johnston, *The Bone Yard*, London: Hodder and Stoughton, 1998, p.261.

11   Alasdair Gray, *A History Maker*, Harmondsworth: Penguin, 1995, p.116.

12   Matthew Fitt, *But n Ben A-Go-Go*, Edinburgh: Luath Press, 2001, p.56.

13   Ibid., p.57.

14   Ibid., pp.63-64.

15 R.L. Stevenson, "The Scot Abroad", in *Silverado Squatters*, The Skerryvore Edition, Vol.16, London: William Heinemann, 1925, p.192.

16 Joy Hendry, "Personal reflections on being Scottish today", in Tom Devine, Paddy Logue (eds.), *Being Scottish*, Edinburgh: Polygon, 2002, p.99.

17 Robert Alan Jamieson, "Sie-Færin/Sea-Faring", in *Nort Atlantik Drift*, 1999 (From the unpublished MS, courtesy of the Author).

18 Christine De Luca, "Airborne over Orkney", in *Voes and Sounds. Poems in English and Shetland dialect*, Lerwick: The Shetland Library, 1995, p.51.

19 Ibid., pp.56-57

20 Angus Calder, in Tom Devine, Paddy Logue (eds.), *Being Scottish*, Edinburgh: Polygon, 2002, p.47.

21 Ray Ryan, *Ireland and Scotland. Literature and Culture, State and Nation, 1966-2000*, Oxford: Clarendon Press, 2002, p.16.

22 Ibid., pp.19-20.

23 Tom Devine, Paddy Logue (eds.), *Being Scottish*, Edinburgh: Polygon, 2002, p.xiii.

24 Lewis Grassic Gibbon, *Sunset Song*, London: Pan Books, 1982, pp. 117-18.

25 Hugh MacDiarmid, "On a Raised Beach", in *The Complete Poems of Hugh MacDiarmid*. Vol.I, Michael Grieve, W.R. Aitken (eds.), Harmondsworth: Penguin, 1985, p.426.

26 Seamus Heaney, "Introduction", in Raymond J. Ross, Joy Hendry (eds.), *Sorley MacLean. Critical Essays*, Edinburgh: Scottish Academic Press, 1986, p.5.

27 Somhairle MacGill-Eain/Sorley MacLean, *O Choille gu Bearradh/ From Wood to Ridge*, Manchester: Carcanet, 1989, pp.226-27.

28   Kenneth White, *The Blue Road*, Edinburgh: Mainstream
     Publishing, 1990, p.29. First published as *La Route Bleue*,
     Editions Grasset et Fasquelle, 1983.

29   Ibid., p.67.

30   Kenneth White, *Geopoetics. Place Culture World*, Edinburgh: Alba
     Editions, 2003, p.5.

31   Alasdair Gray, *Why Scots should Rule Scotland. A Carnaptious
     History of Britain from Roman Times Until Now*, Edinburgh:
     Canongate, 1997, p.1.

32   Ibid., pp. 3-4.

33   Édouard Glissant, *Carribean Discourse: Selected Essays*,
     (translated by J. Michael Dash), Charlottesville: University
     Press of Virginia, 1989, pp. 105-106.

34   C.M. Grieve, *Albyn, or Scotland and the Future*, London: Kegan
     Paul, 1927, p.95.

Index

A page number followed by *n* indicates a reference to the chapter notes. A page number followed by *quot.* indicates a quotation at the beginning of a chapter. Titles of works are given in italics.